PROFESSIONAL DINING ROOM MANAGEMENT

Second Edition

PROFESSIONAL DINING ROOM MANAGEMENT

Second Edition

Carol A. King

JOHN WILEY & SONS, INC.

New York   Chichester   Weinheim   Brisbane   Singapore   Toronto

Designed by Karin Batten

This book is printed on acid-free paper. ∞

This publication is designed to provide accurate and authoritative information in
regard to the subject matter covered. It is sold with the understanding that the
publisher is not engaged in rendering professional services. If professional
advice or other expert assistance is required, the services of a competent
professional person should be sought.

Library of Congress Cataloging-in-Publication Data:

King, Carol A.
Professional dining room management.

Bibliography: p.
Includes index.
1. Restaurant management. 1. Title.
TX911.3.M27K56 1988   647'.95'068   87-29573
ISBN 0-471-28934-5 (pbk.)

Printed in the United States of America

10 9 8

Contents

Preface

This book is written for the forgotten men and women of the restaurant business—the first-line supervisors, specifically those who oversee the service function of the business. Many books, films, and training materials are available that deal with technical aspects of the business: how to wait tables, serve wine, mix drinks, and other aspects of food preparation, as well as management tasks, such as accounting, budgeting, marketing, purchasing, personnel management, and administration. However, few materials are available to assist the supervisor whose staff must meet and serve the public.

The service supervisor's job is a key one in the restaurant business since a large part of the guest's dining experience and satisfaction is derived from the interpersonal contact between guest and staff. If this contact is not satisfactory, all the care and investment in decor, food selection, and preparation are for naught.

Some of the material presented here was first developed for Pannell Kerr Forster & Company's book *Profitable Food and Beverage Management: Operations* by Eric Green, Galen Drake, and Jerome Sweeney (Hayden Book Company, Inc., 1978). For readers seeking a general text on food and beverage operations, that book and its companion volume, *Profitable Food and Beverage Management: Planning* are recommended.

I wish to thank Eric Green and the partners of Pannell Kerr Forster & Company for permission to use their material in this volume. I would also like to thank Tony Aigner for permission to include illustrative material from Windows On The World, The Market Dining Rooms and Bar, and The Corner restaurants.

Dennis Sweeney of The Joseph Baum Company also provided material for the Second Edition.

The English language is a bit cumbersome when it comes to masculine and feminine pronouns. Rather than burden the reader with he/she and waiter/waitress throughout the text, we have used the masculine form.

1

Introduction

In most dining room operations, the ultimate objective is to make a profit, both this year and in the long run. There are some types of table service operations, such as private clubs or executive dining rooms, where the primary objective is to give service to the patron. However, even in a nonprofit situation, the goal is to provide the best possible service for the amount of money spent. There are few, if any, nonprofit organizations these days that can afford to let their operating costs run out of control.

Remember that the objective in commercial restaurants is to remain profitable in the long run. Anyone can make a fast buck by bleeding the business and cheating the customer. To remain profitable a restaurant must offer good value to its customers and job satisfaction to its employees and managers. Why job satisfaction? Because profits are created by people, and having a stable, trained, and motivated staff certainly makes the job easier.

Good value to the customer does not mean cheap prices. It refers to the quality and quantity of food, the level of service, and the decor and ambiance provided for the price paid. There are few real bargains in this world, but the enterprising manager who can offer more to his customers than the competitor down the street will do well.

Good service is one of the primary things people consider in judging value in a restaurant. While good service cannot overcome problems of poor-quality food or sloppy housekeeping, poor service can ruin an otherwise excellent meal for the guest and cost the restaurant considerable goodwill and repeat business.

Regardless of the type of restaurant, good service always has two requirements: efficiency and courtesy. Efficient service does not necessarily mean speed. Rather, it means serving each course at the right time, with the food at the proper temperature, and with all the required accompaniments and utensils. In a coffee shop, efficient service is fast service; in a luxury restaurant, it is service that is timed to allow the guest to enjoy a leisurely meal, with each course served exactly when he is ready for it.

A pleasant, courteous staff can make a strong contribution to the restaurant's overall public image. If the personnel are genuinely interested in providing good service, guests will leave with good feelings about their dining experience.

The restaurant business is a people business, and running a dining room involves a lot more than just bringing in the food and carrying out the dishes. It is really the business of satisfying people's needs—a complicated and demanding goal.

The needs people seek to satisfy when dining out go far beyond basic satisfaction of hunger. They are often looking for status or ego satisfaction, recognition, new experiences, excitement, entertainment, acceptance, and welcome. In fact, the quality of the human relationship is often valued far more than the quality of the food or the decor of the dining room.

Therefore, the first requirement of a good service employee is a customer-oriented attitude; that is, a genuine desire to please the guest. This attitude recognizes that the guest is the reason for being in business and the source of everyone's paychecks. It is not an attitude of demeaning servitude, but rather one of professional hospitality.

The first and most important step toward creating a staff of employees who are customer-oriented is, of course, the selection of the staff, and this is discussed in chapter 13. Once an individual is hired, however, his on-the-job behavior depends to a certain extent on the training provided, but even more so, on the examples set by supervisors and by other employees. Thus, the supervisor is the role model. By both telling the new employee what behavior is expected and demonstrating that type of behavior, the supervisor sets and maintains the standard for the department.

The following are four basic axioms for quality service:

1. The way the supervisor treats guests is the way the staff will treat guests. If the supervisor is cold and abrupt to a guest, the staff will be cold and abrupt also.
2. The value that the supervisor puts on guest service is the value the staff will put on being of service. If the supervisor views other things, such as setting up or ordering supplies, as more important than serving a guest, then so will the staff.
3. The way the supervisor treats the staff is the way the staff will treat each other, and the way they will treat guests.
4. The quality of service that the supervisor expects from the staff is the quality they will provide.

In this book, *quality* and *standards* have quite specific meanings. *Standards* are statements of specific, observable characteristics of job performance. Standards are written down and communicated to employees so that they know exactly what is expected of them as they perform their duties. *Quality* refers to how well an individual's performance meets the standards that have been set.

The title of this book is *Professional Dining Room Management*, but what does it actually mean to be a professional in this business? First, of course, it means mastering the skills of one's calling. But being a professional goes beyond learning a set of skills. It incorporates all of the following as well:

- Having a commitment to the highest standard of performance at all times.
- Having a dedication to one's career and putting the interests of the job first.
- Keeping up with new ideas and trends in the industry.
- Continuing one's education by taking courses, reading books and trade magazines, and visiting other restaurants to see what they are doing.
- Helping others develop their skills and guiding young people in planning their careers.
- Joining professional organizations and working with others in the field for the good of the industry.

How does a dining room manager achieve a professional level of service in his dining room? Good service is not an accident; it does not just happen. It is the result of planning, organization, and supervision. The dining room manager needs four kinds of skills to achieve it:

1. The manager must be a good technician—one who knows the mechanics of serving food.
2. The manager must be a good supervisor—directing, training, and motivating the staff.
3. The manager must be a good customer relations person— able to meet the public and merchandise the restaurant while promoting sales.
4. The manager must be a good administrator—organizing the work flow and controlling costs in his or her department.

This book provides a guide for achieving professional, quality service in the dining room, whether it is a coffee shop or a luxury restaurant. Since there are a number of books available on the technical aspects of service, this book stresses the management and supervisory aspects. In the appendix, you will find a list of good technical books on restaurant service.

2

Types of Dining Room Service

Three types of service are commonly used in restaurants in the United States: French, Russian, and American. Other types that are sometimes used include buffet service for special occasions and parties, family style, and tray service.

FRENCH SERVICE

This style of service is found in restaurants offering classic French cuisine and in other types of operations that cater to a sophisticated clientele (fig. 2-1). French service is distinguished by the fact that all or part of the preparation of the dish, or at least the finishing of it, is done in the dining room. The food is brought from the kitchen on silver platters, carefully arranged and suitably garnished, and presented to the guest for his inspection. The captain or maître d' then completes the prepa-

5

2-1. French service. The waiter prepares the dish on the guéridon at the guest's tableside.

ration on a cart or *guéridon* next to the guest's table. A *rechaud* or alcohol lamp may be used for warming or for last minute sautéing of an item. This finishing is done in the guest's presence and to his exact preference. It offers him not only personalized attention, but also a show, depending on the skill and personality of the staff.

A highly skilled staff is required to give good French service. A captain must know how to bone fish and poultry, carve meats, dress salads, and prepare flaming and chafing dish items. Waiters must be familiar with the ingredients and methods for preparing numerous classic dishes, and busboys must be trained in the proper serving techniques (fig. 2-2).

2-2. French service technique. Holding the service fork and spoon.

Unfortunately, many operators attempt to offer French service without properly training their staff, resulting in service that is a poor imitation of French service at best. It lacks one of the prime ingredients that gives French service its dignity—namely, professionalism. Each detail of true French service is done in consideration of the guest and is not a pointless empty ritual.

French service is very expensive if executed properly and requires a high menu price. A large staff of skilled waiters, captains, and bus help is required. A large inventory of hollow ware must be bought and maintained, as well as a large quantity of flatware, china, and high-quality glassware. Because of the numerous pieces of ware required for the service of each guest, warewashing can also be a major expense. Furthermore, since side tables are required for French service, fewer dining tables can be placed in a given area. French service should not be rushed; usually only one seating can be obtained for each meal. All of these requirements limit the potential sales that can be obtained in a given space.

RUSSIAN SERVICE

Service à la Russe, or Russian service, is a variation of French service (fig. 2-3). The major difference is that, in Russian service, all carving and finishing is done in the kitchen. The individual portions are then arranged on trays or platters and garnished attractively. The waiter carries the tray directly to the table and, after presenting it for inspection, serves the food onto the empty plate before the guest. The advantage of Russian service is that hot food does not get cold while it is being finished in the dining room. This service is most often used for banquets where all the guests are being served at the same time.

AMERICAN SERVICE

In American service all food is plated and garnished in the kitchen. The filled plates are then carried to the dining room and placed before the guest (fig. 2-4). There are many advan-

2-3. Russian service. The veal cutlet has been arranged and garnished in the kitchen.

tages to this type of service, which accounts for its widespread use. The highly skilled French service waiter and captain are not required. Plating and garnishing can be done under the supervision of the chef, and an attractive arrangement of the items and garnishes can be devised. Finally, the food is more likely to be the proper temperature when it is served.

BUFFET SERVICE

Buffet service involves the arrangement of food on platters displayed on large tables (fig. 2-5). Usually a separate table is used for each course. Plates and silverware are conveniently arranged, and the guests serve themselves or are assisted by servers.

2-4. American or plate service. The food has been arranged on the plate in the kitchen and is presented to the guest by the waiter.

2-5. The Grand Buffet Table, Windows On The World. (Photograph Ezra Stoller © Esto. Courtesy of Inhilco and Windows On The World.)

Buffets may be of many types. Weekend brunch buffets are very popular in some areas. A commercial restaurant may offer a special buffet lunch or dinner to boost sales on low-volume days, or it may operate a buffet on a regular basis. One very popular type of service offers appetizers, salad, and breads buffet style, with the rest of the meal served at the table. Occasionally, a luxury restaurant may display menu items—usually appetizers and hors d'oeuvre—on a buffet table. The guest makes his choice, and the items selected are then plated by the waiter and served to the guest at his table. This style of service applies the merchandising aspects of the buffet to fine table service. The elegant display invites the guest to select the items shown, but he is not expected to serve himself; full service is provided. The display is also maintained throughout the meal, since the food is being plated by professional waiters rather than unpracticed guests.

Buffet service is versatile and lends itself to every type of meal, from breakfast to steak roasts. It is very popular for function and group business and may be used for receptions and cocktail hours before a regular table-service banquet. Teas are also a form of buffet service.

OTHER TYPES OF SERVICE

Other types of service are occasionally found in hotels, restaurants, and in some institutional food services. Among them are butler service, family-style service, and tray service.

Butler Service

Butler service is used for stand-up affairs, such as cocktail parties or receptions. White-gloved waiters circulate among the guests, passing finger foods, such as canapés or finger sandwiches, arranged on small silver trays. Champagne is sometimes served butler style at weddings (see fig. 2-6).

Family-Style Service

Family-style service is the presentation of food in bowls or platters that are passed from hand to hand by the guests, who help

2-6. Butler service. Champagne is served at a wedding reception.

themselves as they pass. This type of service is unusual in an urban restaurant, but is suited to a country-style operation that offers a limited menu with unlimited portions for a set price. It is in keeping with an informal, rustic theme. Family service is occasionally found in institutions. In such cases, the residents usually have no choice of entrées.

Tray Service

Tray service was once thought suitable only for feeding the sick. However, with the increasingly sophisticated food services offered on airplanes, it has lost its sickbed connotation and is often referred to as airline service. It is usually used in a fast-service operation with a very limited menu. The server takes the order, goes to a serving pantry, and gathers everything required for the order onto a tray, making only one trip back to the guest. Clearing the table is also fast, requiring only the removal of the tray.

COMBINATION STYLES OF SERVICE

Very often, a mixture of several styles is used. Some entrées may be plated in the kitchen, while others are served as in French or Russian service. A casserole or potpie may be dished onto the plate before the guest in Russian style; a steak may be plated in the kitchen, and a flaming dish prepared on the guéridon. The guest may serve himself the first course from an hors d'oeuvre buffet table, and the rest of the meal may be served to him.

What is important here is not that the service is of several styles, but that the management must plan the details of service to suit the menu, the physical facilities, the kind of clientele, and the seat turnover desired. The staff must then be trained to follow these details.

CLASSIFICATION OF SERVICE BY MEANS OF DELIVERY

Service is sometimes classified by the means used to deliver the food to the guest—cart service, tray service, or arm service. In classic French service, the food may be delivered to the guéridon by cart. This eliminates the carrying of heavy silver service pieces and also provides a place to set the loaded tray. It is also more elegant in appearance. After the finishing step, the plated food is delivered to the guest individually by hand.

Tray service may be of several types. Large trays, called *hotel ovals*, may be used in French or American service to transport food to a side stand. Because of the size of these trays, they are usually heavily loaded and carried over the shoulder. A large tray may be both an advantage and a disadvantage. A number of plates may be carried in one trip, but a waiter who is not particularly service-oriented may be tempted to delay his service until he has a full tray, and thus cut down on the number of trips to the kitchen.

Small trays—either round, oval, or rectangular—are carried on one arm at waist level. These are used for cocktail service and occasionally for American service of food. If properly used, these small trays are never set down. Plates are carried from the kitchen and placed directly on the table from the tray held by the server. This type of tray service is suited to low- and medium-priced operations with a more rapid turnover.

Arm service is usually found in less elegant surroundings, such as diners and coffee shops. Plated food is carried by hand directly to the table. Some servers may be inclined to stack numerous plates of food on their arms to reduce the number of trips. If plate covers are not used, this practice can result in mashed, unappetizing, and unsanitary food.

3
Dining Room Organization

TRADITIONAL DINING ROOM STAFFING

In the European system of staffing, the maître d'hôtel is in charge of the dining rooms and all food and beverage functions, with the exception of those supervised by the chef de cuisine. In a large restaurant or hotel, there may be one or more assistant maîtres d'hôtel who supervise different dining rooms or banquet rooms. Other subordinate management positions include:

- Chef de service—Director of service
- Chef d'etage—Director of service on a floor
- Maître d'hôtel de carre—Supervisor of a section of a dining room

In the dining room, the *chef de rang* (chief of the station or row of tables) is an experienced waiter who takes guests' orders and does the difficult carving and finishing of the dishes. He is responsible for the service in his station. The chef de rang has one or more assistants called *commis de rang*. The commis is a less experienced waiter who brings the food from the kitchen and assists the chef de rang by passing plated food to the guests and clearing the dirty dishes from the table. Before becoming a commis, he served as an apprentice for three years to learn the trade.

The *sommelier*, or wine steward, is in complete charge of the wine cellar. He selects the wines to be stocked by the restaurant and, during service, assists guests in making their wine selections. Actual service of the wine may be performed by the sommelier or by a captain. Occasionally the sommelier supervises a staff of assistants who may serve liquor as well as wines.

In the traditional hierarchy of the French dining room, each position is a training ground for the next higher level. This procedure assures a supply of labor that is well trained in all aspects of good service. It also develops a high level of professionalism in restaurant service and a pride in the profession among restaurant personnel.

STAFFING IN AMERICAN RESTAURANTS

Very few restaurants in the United States are staffed according to the traditional system. There are no apprenticeships or formalized routes for career advancement as there are in the European system. Those in lower-level positions tend to remain in them, resulting in a stratified hierarchy and a general lack of professionalism. The standard job classifications are:

- Maître d'hôtel
- Captain
- Waiter
- Busboy

The maître d'hôtel is responsible for all service in his dining room, although he may delegate direct supervision of service to his captains. He also maintains the reservation book and greets arriving guests at the door. He knows regular guests by name and is ready to provide personal service, knowing in advance their preferences.

In American restaurants offering French service, captains, waiters, and busboys usually work in teams with one captain and one busboy for every two or four waiters. The captain takes the orders and supervises the service in his station. He also performs the carving and finishing of the dishes. The waiters work in pairs, with one serving as runner to the kitchen and the other remaining at the station to attend to the guests. The busboy clears and resets the tables, pours the water, and keeps the station supplied with linen and ware.

For American or plate service, many of the captain's skills are not required, and this position is usually eliminated in a small restaurant or coffee shop.

In a large formal dining room using American service, however, captains are used to supervise the service and the seating in their assigned sections. In such situations, a maître d' is stationed at the door, and ushers are used to direct guests to the various sections of the room, where they are met by the captain. At the table, the captain makes sure the menus are presented, all table appointments are in order, and cocktail orders are taken. Though a waiter may take the order, the captain is responsible for all service in his section. He may also serve wines if a sommelier is not employed. The captain may also be responsible for preparing and presenting the check.

The sommelier position usually exists in an American restaurant that offers French service. If the establishment does not have an extensive wine cellar or a sophisticated clientele, the position may be retained, but then the job is more likely a matter of fetching and serving, with the wine buying done by the manager.

In dining rooms offering fast service, such as a coffee shop, the position of host or hostess is usually found. The duties of the host are not much different from those of the maître d'. The type of service, however, is much less elaborate, and there is less likely to be extensive beverage service. Also, this type of restaurant usually does not accept reservations. In a small restaurant, the host may also be responsible for cashiering.

In a large fast-service restaurant, ushering and seating require the host's full attention during busy periods. In such cases, the duties of this position do not include supervision of service. The host remains at the door, and someone else—a service supervisor, room manager, or assistant manager—assumes the responsibility for the supervision of service. This person is free to move about the dining room to oversee service and is not occupied with seating guests. In such situations, the service supervisor is a management position with full line authority and responsibility for the operation of the room; the host or hostess at the door is a subordinate position, usually without authority over the staff.

JOB DESCRIPTIONS

Following are general job descriptions for dining room supervisory personnel.

Supervisor of Service, Director of Service, or Dining Room Manager

Reports to: General manager or owner.

General Description of Duties: Supervises the operation of all dining rooms, including hiring, training, and scheduling of service personnel. Maintains service standards and oversees the upkeep of physical facilities. Conducts daily lineups of service personnel. Supervises service during serving periods. Handles guest complaints. In conjunction with manager and chef, helps plan menus, controls costs (primarily payroll costs), and works to build sales. Carries out management policies within the department.

Personnel Supervised: Seating host, ushers, captains, waiters, and busboys. May also supervise banquet maître d', coat check and rest room attendants, and wine steward.

Works with: Executive chef, controller or chief cashier; executive steward or back of the house manager; and catering sales manager.

Special Skills and Qualifications: Thorough knowledge of table service techniques (including French service), food, cookery, wines, and liquors. Ability to direct personnel and administer the department. Ability to plan, including forecasting and participation in making budgets. Ability to meet the public and handle complaints and problems.

Comments: Position usually found only in large operations.

Seating Host or Maître d'

Reports to: Director of service.

General Description of Duties: Supervises the handling of reservations and seating of guests in a large restaurant. May supervise greeters, ushers, or telephone receptionist. Books parties in the restaurant and makes special arrangements as required.

Special Skills: Ability to deal with the public in a gracious manner; ability to remember names, faces, and guests' preferences; a knowledge of fine food and wines; ability to present a good appearance; a pleasant speaking voice. May be required to speak more than one language, depending on clientele.

Comments: More often found in large restaurants.

Maître d'

Reports to: General manager or owner.

General Description of Duties: Supervises the overall operation of a formal dining room, including hiring and training of personnel, maintaining service standards, and overseeing the upkeep of physical facilities. Receives reservations, keeps reservation book, greets guests at the door, and supervises seating. May also plan and book private parties. Helps with menu planning and cost control, and works to build sales volume.

Personnel Supervised: Captains, waiters, and busboys. May also supervise the wine steward.

Works with: Chef, chief steward, chief cashier, or controller. May also work with banquet manager if there is a large banquet business.

Special Skills and Qualifications: Thorough knowledge of table service techniques (including French service), food, cookery, wines, and liquors. Ability to direct personnel and administer the department. Ability to deal with the public in a gracious manner; ability to remember names, faces, and guests' preferences; ability to present a good appearance; a pleasant speaking voice. May be required to speak more than one language, depending on clientele.

Comments: More often found in smaller, formal restaurants that do not have directors of service.

Host or Hostess

Reports to: General manager or owner. (May report to a director of service in a multirestaurant complex.)

General Description of Duties: Supervises the operation of a coffee shop or informal table service restaurant. Maintains standards of service and oversees the upkeep of physical facilities. Hires, trains, and schedules staff. Conducts daily lineups of staff, supervises service during meal periods, and handles guest complaints. Oversees the door, seats guests, and controls waiting lines. May also supervise cashiers or act as cashier.

Supervises: Waiters, waitresses, and busboys. May also supervise assistant host or seating host in a large operation.

Special Skills and Qualifications: Ability to meet the public in a gracious manner, supervise the staff, and administer the department. Should be able to handle complaints and problems. Should present a good appearance—neat and well groomed. Some knowledge of food and cookery is usually required, as well as knowledge of table service techniques. Knowledge of alcoholic beverage service may also be required.

4

Quality Service Standards

In the hospitality world, the use of the word *quality* often involves a value judgment in terms of "good" and "bad": "This is a quality operation," or "We sell a quality steak." The problem with such value judgments is that everyone has his own idea of what good and bad quality means. This is not much help to the service supervisor who needs to establish standards. A more systematic approach is needed. Before such a system can be established, though, one must first get rid of the idea that quality is either "good" or "bad." All service has some "quality." The question is, does that quality meet the service supervisor's standard.

THE QUALITY-CONTROL SYSTEM

Many large companies have a *quality-control system* that helps ensure that all output meets predetermined standards. Such a system defines the methods and procedures that are used, and hopefully eliminates waste and inefficiency. The system provides a way of measuring how well the standards are met. When they are not met, it provides a way of identifying the cause of the error, which is the first step toward eliminating it.

The components of such a system are:

1. The establishment of service standards based on guests' needs and expectations.
2. The establishment of internal standards so that the operation will meet the guests' needs and expectations in the most efficient, least costly manner.
3. Written policies and procedures that say *how* things are to be done so that they meet the standards.
4. Performance checking to be sure that the standards are met.
5. When standards are not met, the analysis of poor performance for its cause; and then the correcting of it.

Thus, there are two sides to a service quality-control system: first, satisfying the customers by meeting their needs and expectations; and second, doing it in the most efficient manner, so that the company's profit and productivity objectives are met as well.

In this chapter and throughout this book, you will find frequent reference to standards. A *standard* is a statement of a specific, observable expectation about a performance. Standards are either expressed in measurable terms (for example, *all* guest checks are priced and totaled correctly) or in "yes-no" terms (the lobby floor is free of litter).

A *procedure*, on the other hand, states *how* to perform a specific task. For example:

Serve fruit pie, ⅛-cut, on a 7-inch plate. Place the plate in front of the guest with the point of the pie facing him. Serve a place fork to the left of the plate.

A standard related to this procedure might be worded: Fruit pies are served according to the stated procedure.

Procedures, like recipes, should be written with action verbs: *serve* the plate; *use* tongs to serve the roll; *suggest* to the guest; *place* the fork.

One component of the service quality-control system is checking performance to see that the standards are being met. While many managers rely on their own observation of operations to check performance, a formal quality-control system goes much further. Measurable evaluations of specific standards are sought. The advantage of this approach is that performance can be evaluated over time. Different units of a company can be compared, and managers can be rewarded based on their performance. Finally, feedback to both managers and employees, an important component in any quality program, can be objective and specific.

One technique many companies use in measuring conformance to standards is a checklist. Standards are reworded in the form of questions that can be answered with "yes" or "no," or with quantitative answers: Were the desserts served according to the stated procedures?

Checklists may be used by managers, by inspectors employed by the restaurant company, or by outside shoppers, as described below. When a measurable record is desired, points are assigned to each question on the checklist, and the results are tabulated. A sample service checklist is shown in figure 4-1.

Other measures of conformance to standards are available. External measures include guest complaints, guest comment cards, and outside shopping services. Internal measures of conformance include statistics on labor productivity, sales per employee, and sometimes breakage or usage of supplies.

Guest complaints are an immediate and powerful indicator of how well external quality standards are being met. Complaints made in the dining room during service should be recorded in a logbook for later analysis. (The dining room logbook is discussed in chapter 8.) Complaints made after service (over the phone or by letter) should also be recorded. Although complaints are generally "open-ended" and not measurable, the data can usually be grouped into useful classifications, and critical areas of dissatisfaction can be identified. The number of complaints received on different aspects of service can be tracked over time.

Guest comment cards are widely used, although they have been criticized as being too general and as presenting an unrepresentative picture of the operation. However, they do

4-1. A portion of a checklist used by an outside shopping service to evaluate service.

DINING ROOM SERVICE CHECKLIST

Date: _____ Time: _____ Number in party: _____

Inspector: _____ Dining area: _____

Y/N   Pts

____ _____ Was your reservation made in a courteous and professional manner?

____ _____ Were you seated within 10 minutes of the reserved time?
Comments regarding reservations: _____

Host behavior:

____ _____ Greeted you courteously and promptly on arrival?
____ _____ Addressed you by name?
____ _____ Smiled and made eye contact?
____ _____ Used open body language?
____ _____ Gracious, helpful manner?
____ _____ Pleasant tone of voice?
____ _____ Answered questions courteously and knowledgeably?
____ _____ Neat, well-groomed appearance and correct uniform?
____ _____ Seated your party quickly at a satisfactory table?
____ _____ Checked on service during the meal?
____ _____ Thanked you and invited you back on departure?
Comments: _____

Server(s): _____
Server behavior:

____ _____ Smiled and made eye contact?
____ _____ Greeted you within 2 minutes?
____ _____ Used open body language?
____ _____ Used suggestive selling techniques?
____ _____ Neat, well-groomed appearance and correct uniform?

Service procedures:

____ _____ Were you asked if you wanted cocktails?

(continued)

4-1. *Continued.*

____ _____ Were your cocktails served correctly?
____ _____ Were you presented with the wine list?
____ _____ Were your orders taken promptly?
____ _____ Did the server answer questions about the menu items correctly?
____ _____ Did the server suggest appropriate wines to go with the items ordered?
____ _____ Were the items that you ordered served correctly to each member of your party?
____ _____ Did the server ask "Who gets what?" when serving?
____ _____ Were you served warm rolls and butter as soon as your food order was taken?
____ _____ Were you offered additional rolls during the meal?
____ _____ Were proper accompaniments and service ware served with each menu item?
____ _____ Was each course served in a timely manner, not too soon or too late?
____ _____ Did the server check back after each course was served?
____ _____ Was the preceding course cleared properly before the next course was served?
____ _____ Was the check presented when you were ready for it?
____ _____ Was the check itemized and totaled correctly?
____ _____ Did the server thank you and invite you to return?
Comments: _____
_____
_____
_____

Condition of dining room:

____ _____ Were vacated tables cleared quickly and reset?
____ _____ Was the carpet clean?
____ _____ Was the furniture dusted?
____ _____ Were the windows clean?
____ _____ Were the side stands neat and organized?
____ _____ Was the table set up correctly?
____ _____ Were the table linens clean and in good condition?
____ _____ Was the china, glassware, and silverware clean and polished?
Comments: _____
_____

_____ Total Points

provide some indication of performance and they can produce quantitative data over time.

Complaint analyses and comment cards share a major weakness—both reflect an evaluation of only those customers who took the trouble to respond. To get a more unbiased evaluation, some larger companies use customer surveys. The survey is a market research technique, but it is also very useful in evaluating the quality of performance.

The third method of evaluating conformance to external performance standards is the use of a shopping service. Outside companies send in their personnel to test the performance of the operation, and then report on what they have observed. (The "shopper" is not known to the staff, who think he is a customer.)

STANDARDS OF DINING ROOM SERVICE

In a well-run dining room, the standards of service are clearly defined. These standards include the following:

- The steps of service—procedures for taking orders, delivering food and drinks, and clearing tables.
- The proper table setting for each serving period and sales outlet.
- The details of service—how each menu item is to be served (including the accompanying table ware), merchandising, and selling procedures (discussed in chapter 9).
- Staff behavior and appearance (discussed in chapter 5).

Steps of service, the proper table setting, and the details of service will be discussed in this chapter.

STEPS OF SERVICE

The following are the basic steps necessary in serving a guest:

1. Seating and presenting the menu.
2. Cocktail service, if available.

3. Taking the orders and placing on the table the water, rolls, relishes, or other items required by the style of service.
4. Placing the orders with the kitchen and obtaining them.
5. Preparing and presenting the check and collecting the money.
6. Clearing the table and resetting for the next customer.

Seating and Presenting the Menu

Seating the guests is usually done by a maître d' or host, who also presents the menu (if there is one). If guests seat themselves, the waiter must present the menu. In some fast-service restaurants, the menu is posted on the wall or on a placemat. Some publike restaurants also use a chalkboard or wallboard. The waiter usually draws the guests' attention to it, pointing out the specials or reciting them if they are not listed.

Cocktail and Wine Service

When cocktail service is offered, either the host, the captain, or the server may ask if a cocktail is desired. After the order is taken, the server goes to the bar, places the order, and obtains and serves the drink.

In an establishment with an extensive wine list, wine service is likely to be handled by a separate individual or staff. When a guest requests the wine list, the captain or server summons the wine steward or sommelier to the table, and he takes the order and handles the wine service. In operations with a more limited wine list, the captain or waiter serves the wine.

Chapter 6 describes the steps of wine and beverage service in more detail.

Taking the Orders

In fast-service restaurants, the menu is often posted outside or at the door, and the guest may be ready to give his order as soon as he is seated. Usually, however, the guests like to look over the menu and make their selections at their leisure. While they are doing this, the waiter or busboy can fill the water glasses and serve the butter, breads or crackers, relishes, or any other items required by the style of service. When the guest turns his attention from the menu, he is ready to give his order.

Orders may be written directly on a guest check, on a special preprinted form, or on a captain's order pad. Orders are usually taken from the ladies first. The system described for taking drink orders can also be used for taking food orders. If the whole staff uses the same system, any waiter can serve an order taken by another. This is especially important when waiters work in teams.

To speed order taking and minimize errors, a common set of abbreviations should be established. One code, known to and used by all, is essential to the quick and accurate preparation of orders by the cooks. A standard code also makes the auditing of checks easier and more accurate.

Sometimes items are numbered on the menu for fast ordering. If numbers and abbreviations are used on the guest check, they should give sufficient indication of what the item is, so the guest can tell for what he is being charged.

Placing the Orders with the Kitchen and Obtaining Them

Orders must be transmitted clearly to the kitchen to avoid errors or misunderstandings. If some items must be prepared to order, the waiters should know how long these orders take and co-ordinate them so that the entire party's order will all be ready at the same time. In many of the busier kitchens, the chef or his assistant does this coordinating or expediting at the range. (In the French kitchen, this position is known as the *abboyeur*, or barker.) The expediter receives the written orders from the waiters and gives them to the proper stations, such as the broiler cook, roast cook, fry cook, or vegetable cook. The expediter also coordinates the timing of the various orders, approves the dishes going out, and provides some control by seeing that no food is dispensed without being recorded on a guest check.

After the waiter has put in his orders at the range, he assembles his first-course orders on his tray, drawing the hot soups last so that they are still hot when served. If no appetizers or soups are ordered, the salad is sometimes served in its place, especially if the entrée is prepared to order.

The waiter may dish up and garnish some items himself. Spoons, tongs, and forks should always be used to handle food. The service procedure should specify the portion sizes for items dished up by waiters. Some waiters mistake generous portions for good service and think that serving extra-large helpings of rolls, butter, cream, jelly, and so forth will increase their tips. The dining room supervisor should be alert to waste of this nature. Management should establish a policy on the service of extra-large helpings—how much is to be served when requested and what, if anything, is to be charged for such requests.

When picking up orders in the kitchen, all cold items should be picked first; hot foods, last. The tray should be loaded so that the weight is balanced. Whenever possible, the items should be arranged in order of the service. For American service, the entrées should be covered and stacked in the same order in which they will be served. This procedure will provide quick, efficient service with a minimum of delay, thus preventing hot food from getting cold. All accompanying items should be collected and taken on the same trip. It helps if things that are served together are kept together. This saves steps and time. The waiter does not have to return to the kitchen for a forgotten fork or sauce, while the guest sits looking at his food.

The organization of one's tray and one's station should be stressed when training new waiters. Before leaving his station to go to the kitchen, the waiter should check the progress of each party and anticipate its needs. If one group is almost finished with the appetizers, they may be ready for the main course before the waiter returns from the kitchen. If the orders are ready, they can be brought immediately. This is what is meant by organization of the station. As the cliché goes, "Use your head and save your feet."

Preparing and Presenting the Check and Collecting the Money

In many operations, the check must be made out and properly priced before the waiter can pick up his orders from the range.

This is known as prechecking. There are various other methods of controlling guest checks and cash. Since this is an important aspect of internal control, it is discussed separately in chapter 17.

Clearing the Table and Resetting for the Next Customer

The faster the table is cleared and reset after the guest has left, the sooner the next party can be seated. In some establishments, clearing is left solely to the bus help. A smart waiter knows that the faster his tables are reset, the more guests he can serve and the more tips he will make. Where union regulations permit, waiters should be encouraged to bus their own tables whenever they can. Taking dirty dishes when going to the kitchen does not take any more time than going with an empty tray. Furthermore, uncleared tables are unsightly and detract from the appearance of the dining room.

In some types of operations, guests may be seated at uncleared tables. This should only be done when it cannot be avoided—as in fast-turnover, high-volume operations such as coffee shops.

The proper way to clear or bus a table should be established. If silverware is separated and plates scraped and stacked as the table is cleared, dishwashing becomes much more efficient, and breakage costs are reduced. Noise levels in the dining room are also lowered.

When the tablecloth is changed during service, it should be done discreetly, without a flourish that could be distracting to nearby guests. The correct way to change a tablecloth is to fold back one edge of the soiled cloth and position the clean cloth on the uncovered edge of the table. The soiled cloth is then folded as the clean cloth is unfolded in position on the table. Crumbs are wrapped in the soiled cloth rather than shaken onto the floor or seats (fig. 4-2).

Tablecloths are always changed without exposing the unclothed table top and without placing anything on the chairs. The following is a sample procedure for changing a tablecloth:

1. As soon as the guests have left, set the tray on the side stand next to the table. The fresh tablecloth should be tucked under your arm to avoid making a second trip.

4-2. How to change a tablecloth. (Courtesy of The Market Dining Rooms and Bar and Inhilco.)

2. Remove everything from the table. Place all glassware, dishware, silverware, and linen on the bus tray. (Be sure to remove glasses without handling the rims or insides.)
3. Pull the table out if it is against a wall.
4. Take into your hands the fresh, folded tablecloth (which should have been under your arm as you did the above).
5. Partially unfold the fresh cloth; hold it at the ends.
6. Reach over the table and grasp the ends of the soiled cloth (sides opposite you).
7. In one motion, slide the soiled cloth off and lay the fresh cloth without exposing the table surface.
8. Roll up the soiled cloth into a tight, neat roll.
9. Put the soiled cloth on your arm.
10. Straighten out the fresh cloth so it is hanging evenly on all sides.
11. Move the table back in place.
12. Wipe the salt and pepper shakers and place them on the clean cloth with the clean ashtray.
13. Remove crumbs from the seats (using the rolled cloth) into your hands, never on the floor.
14. Put the rolled cloth on the tray and remove the tray and side stand.
15. Bring settings to the table—dishware, silverware, and napkins in one hand; glass stems in the other hand. Learn to carry everything in one trip.
16. Set the table.

Note: *Never* bring fresh settings to the table before you have changed the tablecloth because you will have no place to set them down. *Nothing should be placed on chairs.*[1]

TABLE SETTINGS

For many years etiquette has dictated the correct way of setting a table. Although standards of etiquette change over time, people have come to look for certain table implements in certain places. Minor variations can be devised to suit the merchan-

[1]Courtesy of The Market Dining Rooms and Bar and Inhilco.

dising plan of a certain restaurant, but they should not be too different from the accepted pattern. Figures 4-3, 4-4, 4-5, and 4-6 illustrate four styles of table setting—formal, continental, banquet, and informal.

If tablecloths are used, a silence pad is put on the table first. This is a cloth of felt or other thick material that cushions the surface and muffles the sound of china and silver on the table top. Some table tops are covered with a cushioned plastic that serves the same purpose. In many restaurants an undercloth is also used to hide the less presentable silence pad when the cloth is changed during the meal period. In addition, by using a larger undercloth, the top cloth can be smaller, thus saving on laundry costs.

The dining room supervisor is responsible for seeing that there is an adequate supply of table linen of the proper sizes. He may deal directly with the laundry in placing orders, or he may give his order to a steward, housekeeper, or manager.

Paper placemats and napkins may be used in place of linen. Some fast-service operations even eliminate the placemats and put all the silverware on the napkin. Putting silverware directly on the bare table is not an acceptable sanitary practice.

Placemats are usually set about 2 inches from the edge of the table, and any art work or reading matter on them should face the guest. Napkins, either paper or linen, should be placed so that one corner is facing the guest. In this way, he can pick up the open corner, open the napkin, and place it on his lap with one hand.

In years past, napkin folding was an art and in the late nineteenth century, food and table appointments became very ostentatious. Napkins were folded into all sorts of intricate shapes, such as fans, flowers, swans, and hats. An intricately folded napkin can add to an attractive and distinctive table, but folding can be a time-consuming operation and, at today's labor wage rates, very costly.

The space and utensils for each person are called a *cover*. Sufficient space should be allowed for each cover so that the guest is not crowded and can be served promptly. At least 24 inches of space should be allowed. The arrangement of the items required for the cover should be balanced and attractive.

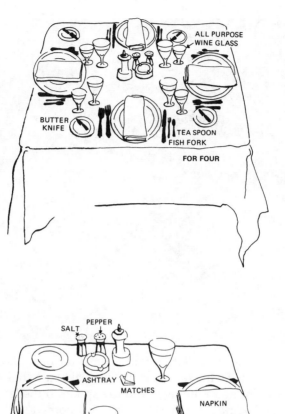

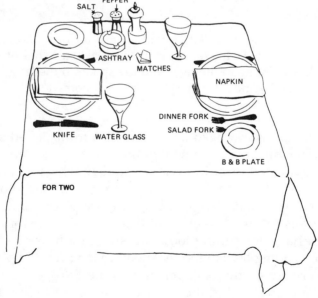

4-3. Formal table setting. (Courtesy of The Market Dining Rooms and Bar and Inhilco.)

4-4. A continental table setting for a formal banquet. A dessert fork and spoon are above the service plate, parallel to the edge of the table; the fork is pointing to the right and the spoon to the left. (Courtesy of Inhilco and Windows On The World Ballrooms.)

Silverware is arranged about 2 inches from the edge of the table. The accepted placement of the knives, forks, and spoons is based on the European style of eating in which utensils used with the left hand (fork) are placed on the left and those used with the right hand (knife and spoon) are placed on the right. Americans eat in a less efficient manner, with the fork held in the left hand for cutting food and switched to the right hand for transporting the food to the mouth. However, the placement of silverware on the table remains in the European style. The pieces are arranged in the order of use, starting from the outside.

The pieces of china, glassware, and silver set for each place are included in the term *cover*. (See figures 4-7, 4-8, and 4-9.) The pieces used depend on the requirements of the meal period,

4-5. A table set for a formal banquet. (Photograph Ezra Stoller © Esto. Courtesy of Inhilco and Windows On The World.)

the type of menu being served, and the type of service offered. Different standard settings may be used for different meal periods. For a formal dinner service or for a very formal luncheon or breakfast service, a service or "show" plate is used. This highly decorative plate is not used for food service, although a cocktail or plated appetizer may be put on top of it. The service plate is removed before subsequent courses are served. The only other china in the American formal setting is the bread and butter plate. (The use of other china and ware depends on the food being served and is brought at the time it is needed.) In operations using a single type of wine glass, the wine glass is part of the cover. If different types of wine glasses are used for different types of wine, the glass is not presented until the wine is served.

For the formal à la carte setting, only basic flatware pieces— a place knife and fork and bread and butter knife are laid. In

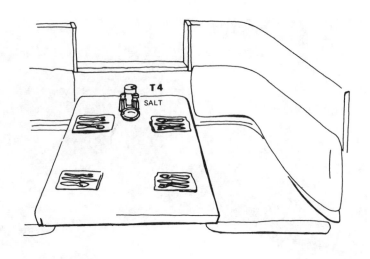

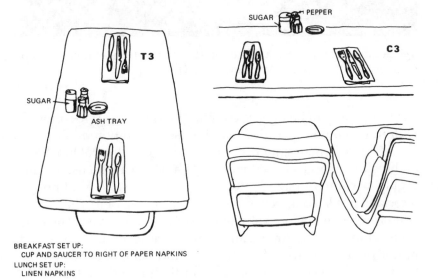

4-6. Informal table setting. (Courtesy of The Corner and Inhilco.)

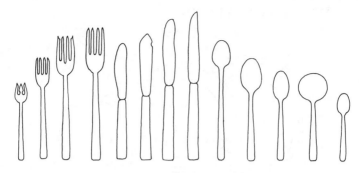

4-7. Commonly used flatware. Left to right: Cocktail or oyster fork, salad fork, fish fork, place fork, butter spreader, fish knife, place knife, steak knife, iced tea spoon, soup or dessert spoon, teaspoon, bouillon spoon, demitasse spoon.

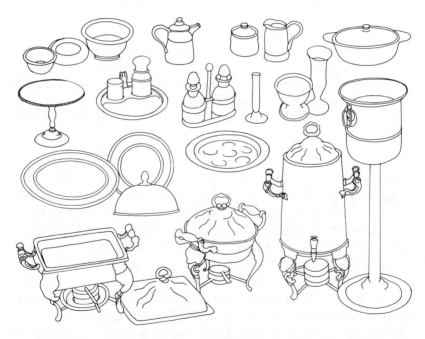

4-8. Hollow ware pieces. Top row, left to right: supreme dish with insert and top, individual coffeepot, creamer and sugar bowl, covered vegetable serving dish; second row: cake stand, oyster condiment tray, vinegar and oil cruets, bud vase, ice cream dish, and parfait dish; third row: oval and round serving platters with a cloche lid, oyster plate; bottom row: rectangular and round chafing dishes with lids, coffee urn, wine cooler with stand.

4-9. Commonly used china pieces. Top row, left to right: 10-inch dinner plate, 9-inch luncheon plate, 7-inch salad plate, 5-inch bread and butter plate; bottom row: service plate with crest, sauce boat, oval steak platter, soup or cereal bowl, soup or pasta plate, side or vegetable dish, bouillon cup with underliner, coffee cup and saucer, demitasse cup and saucer.

formal European settings, a fish fork and a dessert spoon (slightly larger than a teaspoon) are placed above the place setting, parallel to the edge of the table. Other pieces of flatware are carried to the table on a small tray covered with a napkin, after the guest has made his selections from the menu.

For a less formal restaurant or coffee shop, the minimum flatware setting consists of the place fork, place knife, and teaspoon. However, specialty restaurants are more apt to set more pieces—salad fork, extra teaspoon or bouillon spoon, depending on the menu offered. In a steak house, a steak knife may be included in the standard setting. Other pieces of flatware are only served with a particular menu item, such as iced tea or parfait spoons, or cocktail forks. An additional fork is served with pie, and an additional teaspoon with coffee or tea.

For breakfast service, cups and saucers are often part of the place setting for informal restaurants; most people drink coffee or tea for breakfast and want fast service. For lunch and dinner, coffee shops usually dispense with bread and butter plates, but in medium-priced restaurants they are usually set. In fast-service luncheon operations, rolls are typically only served with hot entrée items or with large salads. In that case, the roll is served on the bread and butter plate with the entrée.

A center setup for a coffee shop or less formal restaurant consists of sugar bowl, ashtray and matches (in smoking sections only), salt and pepper shakers, and sometimes a bud vase or condiment bottles. Sugar bowls and salt and pepper shakers are placed in the center of a table that seats four, and along one side of tables for two. If the table for two is a wall table, the side toward the wall is the one used. If it is not a wall table, the side away from the main traffic aisle is used for this purpose.

Ashtrays stocked with matches belong next to the sugar bowls. When the table is cleared, the ashtrays should be cleaned and restocked with matches whenever necessary. If the ashtrays are used, they must be replaced with clean ones as often as necessary during the meal.

In formal à la carte service, accompaniments, such as sugar bowls and condiments, are placed on the table as needed, and then removed.

DETAILS OF SERVICE

The details of service should be spelled out for each item on the menu. If there are special orders (nonlisted items) that are frequently served, instructions should be included for these items as well.

These details of service should be compiled and given to each trainee and also posted at the appropriate point in the kitchen and pantry. Dining room supervisors should review the details of service at lineups from time to time and should be alert to an incorrect service during meal periods. Improper service should be corrected in the kitchen, obviously, and not in the presence of the guests.

Following are several examples of service details.

Soup—Cup

Serve one ladle of soup, dipped from the bottom of the pot, into a soup cup. Follow the instructions given in lineup for garnishing. Serve on a saucer for an underliner. Serve a bouillon spoon. Be sure there are crackers in the roll basket, and offer another basket if there are none.

Soup—Plate

Serve one and one-half ladles, dipped from the bottom of the pot. Use an eight-inch underliner and serve with a soup spoon. Follow other directions for a cup of soup.

Shrimp Cocktail

Fill supreme dish with crushed ice, cover with ring, and place insert dish in the ring. Be sure the cocktail has five shrimp. Use a seven-inch underliner with paper doily. Serve one lemon wedge on the underliner. Be sure there are crackers in the roll basket. Offer another basket if there are none.

Salad, Tossed Green

Served in a wooden bowl. Place a salad-dressing rack on the table when salads are served.

Entrées

Eight-inch plates are used at lunch; 9-inch at dinner. Garnishes will be specified at lineup for the daily entrées. All hot plates are to be covered when taken to the dining room. Some standard items to include with entrées are these:

- *For Lamb chops.* Mint sauce in a relish boat and steak knife. Mint jelly available on request.
- *For Steaks.* Steak knife. Steak sauce available on request.
- *For Chopped steak.* Catsup in a relish boat on request.

Pies

Served on 7-inch liner. Set the piece of pie so the point faces the guest. Serve a place fork.

Ice Cream

Served in an ice cream dish. Use a 7-inch underliner with paper doily. Put one cookie on the underliner. Serve a place spoon.

Coffee

Serve individual pots of coffee for each order. Offer to pour the first cup. Serve a small pitcher of cream for one or two guests and a large pitcher for three or four.

BANQUET SERVICE STANDARDS

Banquet service has some additional performance requirements. Timing and coordination with the kitchen are critical. Nothing kills repeat sales in the banquet business faster than slow, uncoordinated service. Banquet sponsors often go to great efforts and expense in planning their program; having the dessert plates cleared during a major speech or having to cut the program short because of a delay in service is reason to take their event elsewhere in the future.

The steps of service will vary, depending on the menu structure and the nature of the items. For some events, the appetizer and salad may be placed on the table before the guests enter the room. For courses that are served, the head table is always served first; after that, the rest of the tables are served as quickly as possible, so that the lag between service to the head table and the last table is minimized. As each course is completed, it is cleared, along with all accompaniments. Dessert service can be a part of the entertainment, with a long line of waiters emerging from the kitchen doors with flaming trays held aloft.

The table setting will depend on the items to be served, but only the pieces actually required by the menu are set. (Exception: a knife is always set, whether the menu warrants it or not, since it is required by the European style of eating.) Sugar bowls and creamers are usually not placed on tables until coffee is served; salt and pepper shakers are removed before dessert.

Two methods of control are usually used for banquet service. For large groups, attendees will have tickets to the event. These tickets are collected by the waiter or banquet captain. The ticket count determines the number of entrées issued to each waiter, and will verify the billing. For smaller groups, a count is made by the banquet captain or headwaiter and confirmed with the sponsor of the event. In either case, it is essential that counts are communicated to the kitchen for effective control of food and billings.

BUFFET SERVICE STANDARDS

Buffet service also has some unique service requirements. Some buffets are planned so that the guest helps himself to all dishes offered, taking as much as he wishes. With others, hot entrées are served by attendants, while the guest serves himself the other menu items. Whether or not servers are used depends on the speed of service desired, the amount of control needed over multiple choices, and the amount of food served.

For true buffet services, the guest carries his plate in his hand. Some permanent buffet operations offer lavish buffet-type displays, but provide the guests with trays and a tray rail. This type of service is easier for the guests and reduces the possibility of accidents, but is not as elegant as the decorated linen-draped buffet table. The use of trays and the permanent counter installation is closer to a cafeteria operation than to a buffet.

Whether guests serve themselves or are served, personnel are needed to maintain the table, keeping it supplied with plates and freshly filled bowls and platters. Since the buffet's major attraction is its eye-appeal, this is a very important function. Dishes should be refilled before they are half empty. Generally, when the items are set up, at least two dishes are prepared of every item; the second dish is reserved for replenishing. This way, the second, full dish is set in the place of the partially empty dish, and the table never has an empty space or a shortage of food. The partially empty dish is then refilled and held in the kitchen until needed. Toward the close of the meal period, the food on display should be as attractive for the latecomers as it was for the first guest served.

The amount of service rendered to guests at their seats can also vary. Guests may be served only beverages at their tables, or they may be served everything except salads and relishes. Waiters may carry the guests' plates to the tables and bring refills from the buffet, or they may merely clear the dishes from each course as the guests return to the tables for the next course. In any case, the dining room staff should be alert to the needs of feeble or disabled guests and assist them at the buffet as necessary.

The selection of menu items to be offered on a buffet and the method of presenting the items is usually the responsibility of the chef. Whether or not the chef's department is responsible for providing the buffet servers or maintaining the display during service depends on the organization of the restaurant.

BREAKDOWN OF SERVICE

When standards of service are not met, a *breakdown* in service has occurred. There are a number of causes of breakdowns, many of which are not the fault of the waiter.

Poor Seating

When a waiter's station is all seated at once, he may get "stuck" through no fault of his own. If seating is staggered, he can devote attention to each table in turn. There are times, however, when it is impossible to avoid seating a full station, or even a whole dining room, in a very short period. Most guests are willing to wait if their presence is acknowledged by the server. He may say, "Good evening, I'll be with you in just a moment."

No one likes to be ignored. The supervisor should be alert to potential breakdowns caused by the seating pattern and should get help for the waiter.

Physical Layout Problems

Bottlenecks in the kitchen may be a cause of service breakdowns. If the kitchen is a long way from the dining room, team service may be required. This way, at least one waiter is on the station at all times to attend to the guests.

Sometimes only minor changes in the kitchen layout will eliminate a serious bottleneck. If this is not possible, it may be desirable to move some activities that create the bottleneck. For example, waiters could use carts to drop off dirty dishes instead of having to carry them to a congested dishwashing area, or the coffee-making function could be moved to the dining room with single-pot brewing equipment instead of one large coffee station.

Shortage of Ware

Some managers feel they save money by operating with a shortage of silver, china, and glassware. This is a bad practice. It can cause poor staff morale and poor service to the guest. Waiters may resort to carrying silverware and other equipment in their pockets—an unsanitary and unprofessional practice. They may also take it from each other's station, bribe busboys and warewashers, or resort to washing their own ware. This last practice is the least desired of all. It takes the waiter's time when he should be attending to his guest. In addition, he cannot achieve the same level of sanitation as machine washing.

Poor Communication with the Kitchen

When orders are given verbally to the kitchen, there is always a chance for error. Items can be misordered, misunderstood, not heard at all, or completely forgotten. When cooks take orders directly from the waiters, there could be a deliberate foulup, if there is a personality conflict. Many operations, especially larger ones, use electronic cash-register systems that have re- mote printing devices. These automatically print the order in the kitchen after the waiter has entered it into the terminal. Since the terminology is standardized in the computer, there is less chance of a misunderstanding. Also, the computer pro- vides an audit trail, which includes the time the order was en- tered. This can be very useful in checking on speed of service.

Waits or Runouts

Delays in preparation or runouts of food are beyond the control of the dining room supervisor. He can only insist that the kitch- en communicate this information to the waiters as quickly as possible and that the waiters report to the guests for a possible change of orders. Most kitchens use a blackboard for posting the status of items during the meal period. Frequent problems of runouts or delays should be referred to management for cor- rection.

Accidents

Accidents are inevitable, but they can be kept to a minimum by a staff that is trained to be safety conscious. Spills should be wiped up immediately and floors kept clean. Nonskid sur- faces can be installed on floors that are particularly hazardous, such as in dishrooms or on ramps.

Personnel should be trained to announce their presence when passing others loaded with trays and should use such phrases as "passing please," "behind you," or "hot coffee."

When an accident has occurred that will delay service, the supervisor should inform the guest and offer apologies to avoid dissatisfaction. Most guests will be understanding if they know the reason for the delay.

5

Service Staff Behavior and Appearance Standards

While a long list of "thou shalt nots" can be a source of poor morale, certain standards of staff behavior are expected in good service. Smoking, eating, drinking, and gum chewing while on duty should not be allowed. When not busy with service, waiters should be at their stations and alert to the needs of their guests. They should not be permitted to congregate in the kitchen or a corner of the dining room, where loud conversation can be distracting to nearby guests.

Food is not appetizing if served by a person who is slovenly or unclean. Uniforms must be clean and well pressed. Lightweight uniforms should be changed daily. If food is spilled on uniforms, some provision should be made for quick changes. Hands and fingernails should be clean and well groomed. Hair should be clean and neatly styled. Long, loose hair arrangements have no place in a food-service operation. Most Departments of Health require caps or hair nets for food-service workers. Daily baths or showers are necessary, and the use of a deodorant cannot be stressed too firmly. Good dental care is also important. Breath sweetener or mouthwash should be used before going on duty and after smoking.

These standards for behavior and appearance may seem an annoyance or a bore to some staff members, or so basic that they need not even be said. Individually, they are small matters. However, taken all together, they add up to an overall picture or image of a restaurant that guests will remember.

Service is an intangible. Guests cannot taste it or look at it to form an evaluation of it. They make their judgments on what they see and experience, and service personnel who are sloppily dressed or who stand around gossiping will not provide an image of a professionally run operation. Dirty uniforms imply a dirty kitchen. In short, a staff that is not attentive to its guests is saying "We don't want your business." Actions speak louder than words.

COURTESY

The word *courtesy* once referred to certain behaviors that were required in royal courts to show respect for royalty and the upper social classes. Later, courteous behavior became identified with manners and "good breeding."

In today's democratic society, courtesy is still a way of showing respect for others, regardless of their social position or relationship. Courteous behavior shows care and concern for the other person. Some people lament that what was called "common courtesy" has become "uncommon courtesy"; that good manners do not exist any more.

At times, they are right. We have all experienced discourteous or at least apathetic service. When the pace of business is hectic, courtesy can be forgotten. Sometimes, a service person thinks that courtesy is demeaning, or a bunch of meaningless words, or that there is not enough time to be courteous.

For the service professional, courtesy is not something to do when there is time for it. Courtesy is the underlying principle of giving service. If one cannot show respect for those who patronize the business, then he does not deserve their business.

Courteous behavior does more than show respect, though. It has been described as the "lubricant of human relationships." It reduces the frictions that can arise in any interaction, and it helps to keep actions and behaviors on a level at which they can be managed and predicted. Courteous behavior yields courteous reactions.

Courtesy should not be limited to interactions with guests. Courteous behavior toward coworkers also produces courtesy in return, which makes the job a lot more pleasant. It is also much easier to be courteous to the guests in an atmosphere of all-around courtesy.

Courtesy is more than words and phrases, although the words and phrases are important. Courtesy is also expressed through informal communication channels, and these are discussed in chapter 10. Courtesy is also action. It is doing something a little extra—being helpful; perhaps checking back to see if everything is going well for a patron or coworker.

6

Beverage Service Standards

Standards for beverage service follow the same pattern as those for the service of food:

- The steps of service: procedures for taking orders, obtaining the drinks or wine from the bar or wine cellar, serving them, and collecting the payment.
- The details of service: specifying the contents of each drink and how it is to be served.
- Merchandising and selling procedures (covered in chapter 9).
- Server behavior, which is discussed throughout this book. However, with the current public concern about drunk driving, responsible alcoholic beverage service requires more than just the dispensing of drinks. Servers must be able to deal with patrons who are intoxicated and to cut off or slow down service to those who are becoming intoxicated. In chapter 7, Jim Peters (executive director of the Responsible Hospitality

Institute) describes some of the techniques of responsible beverage service. Beverage-server training is discussed in chapter 13.

Beverage service operations are sometimes divided into two functions: bar service and full-bottle wine service. In a very large operation, these may be two separate departments; in smaller restaurants, full-bottle wines are obtained from the bar, but the service techniques are different.

STEPS OF SERVICE: BAR SERVICE

When taking orders for drinks, the server usually does not have a printed drink menu to which to refer (although sometimes specialty drinks may be promoted on the menu or on table tents). Furthermore, in beverage service, guests frequently have favorite drinks and want their cocktails "built" or mixed to order. Therefore, servers should also know the contents of all commonly ordered cocktails and the various ways that they can be served. In addition, the server must know what liquors, beers, wines, and nonalcoholic beverages are stocked at the bar, and the prices for each.

Every bar operation has a "house" or "well" brand for each type of liquor that is poured for mixed drinks and for highballs when the guest does not specify a brand. The server should know what the house brand is in each category. Other brands are "call" brands—brands that the guests ask for by name. Generally, call brands are grouped by management in price categories, which makes it easier for servers and bartenders to remember the prices. Two or three price groups are commonly used; these are often referred to as "regular" or "premium," and occasionally, "top shelf."

The procedure for placing orders at the bar varies according to the method of checking and cashiering and the physical layout.

In a small lounge in which the bartender services both the public bar and the lounge servers, the waiter calls the order to the bartender, who fills it and records it on a check. The checks remain at the bar until the guest is ready to pay.

In larger operations, and especially when drinks are served in a dining room, servers obtain their drinks from a service bar. They may ring up their drinks on a check, which is then presented to the bartender to be filled. Bartenders are instructed never to give out a drink that is not first pre-rung on a check; once they have filled the order, they tick it off on the check. Some of the electronic point-of-sale equipment now on the market can print duplicate checks either remotely at the bar, or at the terminal. The server then turns the duplicate in to the bar to get the order.

When bar orders are written, it is useful to establish a standard set of abbreviations that both waiters and bartenders understand. For example:

Bourbon	B
Scotch	S
Canadian Club	CC
Rum	RUM
Martini	MART
Manhattan	MAN
On the Rocks	R
Twist	T
Water	W
Soda	S

Drink orders would then be written up as follows:

Scotch and water with a twist	S/W/T
Bourbon and soda	B/S
Martini on the rocks	MART/R

This saves time in writing and reduces the possibility of misunderstandings about the order.

It is helpful to the bartender if the orders, either written or oral, are grouped according to type of drink—all highballs called together, mixed drinks, beers, and so on. Some electronic point-of-sale equipment print items in a predetermined order, regardless of how they were entered into the system.

In small operations, the bartenders usually have all necessary supplies and glassware behind the bar (see fig. 6-1). In a high-volume operation, glassware and mixers (soda, quinine, tonic, etc.) may be stored outside of the bar area, so that they can be replenished during service without the runners having to go behind the bar. (Runners, or "bar boys," replenish supplies and glassware, and may even wash glasses.) With such an

6-1. Bar glassware. Top row, left to right: stem cocktail, beer pilsner, champagne flute, all-purpose wine glass, whiskey sour, brandy snifter, coupe, cordial; bottom row, left to right: shot glass, highball, rocks, beer stein.

arrangement, waiters pick up the glassware needed for their order and give it to the bartender. They may also draw the mixers from the soda system or pick up soda splits (individual bottles of mixers). Regardless of which system is used, waiters generally garnish their drinks themselves; that is, they add the olives, cherries, and onions, as well as the stirrers. Thus, training for beverage service should include information on types of glassware in use and the garnishing of various types of cocktails.

In lounges, the usual practice is to keep the tables bare, except for an ashtray and perhaps a lamp or candle. Bar food, such as pretzels or nuts, is placed on the table when the order is taken.

Proper beverage service is performed with a small, round cocktail tray held flat on one hand and wrist (see fig. 6-2). The tray is used even if only one or two drinks are being carried. A small stack of cocktail napkins is carried on the cocktail tray. A napkin is put down on the table first, and then the drink glass is put on top of it.

The service of cocktails or mixed drinks is fairly standard, but highballs may be served several different ways. The liquor and mixer may be put together in the glass at the bar, then presented to the guest. A nicer service is to serve the liquor separately in a shot glass, with the ice and mixer in the highball glass. An even more elegant service is to serve a glass of ice and a split of mixer or water "back" (in a separate glass or pitcher). When liquor is served in a shot glass, the server should ask the guest if he wants it mixed. If the guest does, the shot is poured into the highball glass on the tray before the glass is put on the cocktail napkin. Then, the empty shot glass is taken away. If the guest says "no," the glass is put on the cocktail napkin and the shot of liquor and the mixer, if served separately, are put on the table next to the glass.

To beer drinkers the test of the service is the head; and there is a special technique for pouring bottled beer to get that head. If the guest wants his beer poured, the glass is placed on the table, then the beer poured straight into the center of the glass, with the bottle or can at a steep angle. As the level of beer rises in the glass, the head will form. Then the angle of the bottle is

6-2. Cocktail service. The tray is carried on the hand and wrist.

lowered until it is level, and the glass is filled slowly until the foam is just above the top of the glass. The partially empty bottle or can is left on the table.

Empty glasses and bottles should be removed from the table promptly. If the ashtray is full, it should be removed and a clean one provided. The technique in removing a dirty ashtray is to place a clean one upside down on the dirty one, and then pick them up together. The dirty ashtray is put on the serving tray and then the clean one is put on the table (right side up, of course). This keeps the ashes from flying all over the table.

Formerly many operations had service standards that called for taking orders for refills when glasses were one-third empty. With increasing awareness of the third-party liability issue, however, more leeway on speed of serving refills is now being given. Purposely slowing service to a group that has already had several rounds is one preventive technique. However, guests who are still in the "safe" range should not have to fight to get refills.

The cocktail server should not have to ask who gets which drink. One system for keeping track of orders is to establish one point in the room, such as the door, as a starting base. All seats facing that point are designated as number one, with the other seats numbered clockwise around the table. Orders are written on a scratch pad in order of the seat numbers; not in the order they were taken. For example, if the guests at seats number two and number four are women, their orders can be taken first, but are designated on the scratch pad according to the seat numbers. At the bar, the server calls the order in the proper ordering sequence, and, when picking up the order, rearranges it on the cocktail tray according to the seat number order. Women may still be served first, but the server knows by the order of the drinks on the tray which guest gets which drink.

The procedure for collecting for beverage service varies according to the type of operation. Drinks served in the dining room before a meal are carried on the dinner check. In systems with mechanical checking systems, beverages are recorded on the back of the guest check. Waiters have been known to forget to carry the beverage total forward, resulting in a revenue loss that could be substantial. With electronic point-of-sale equipment, beverage amounts are included automatically when the check is totaled.

In lounges several different systems are used. In a high-volume operation, the policy is frequently "pay when served"; guests are not permitted to run up a tab. If the policy is to permit guests to run up a tab, additional rounds of drinks are run on the same check. If the bartender rings the checks, he retains them until the guest pays, and then cashes out of the bar register.

A few establishments, especially large ones, use lounge cashiers to ring and settle checks for drinks served at tables. This practice is dying, though, because of the added labor cost involved and because the added security of electronic point-of-sale systems makes it unnecessary. Where a lounge is connected to a restaurant operation, servers may settle checks with the restaurant cashier. Another frequently used method requires servers to be their own cashier. Each server is given a "bank" with which to make change. At the end of the shift, the server is responsible for turning in the amount of cash or charge slips recorded against his server number in the register.

STEPS OF SERVICE: WINES

When wine service standards are stated separately from beverage service, they usually refer to full-bottle table wine service. Fortified wines, such as ports and sherries, aperitifs, and wines by the glass or carafe are served from the bar or service bar and accounted for as beverage.

Full-bottle wines are served in the dining room with a meal, although guests may occasionally order a bottle of wine, especially champagne, in a lounge. This practice is growing in some areas where the trend toward "grazing" in the lounge (ordering small portions of different menu items, such as appetizers or side dishes, rather than eating a full meal) is popular.

The procedure for presenting the wine list varies. Restaurants that have a small selection of wines may include the list right on the menu. Others print a small list that is presented with the food menu. Restaurants with an extensive wine cellar may have two wine lists—one short one that lists the selections that are being promoted, and a larger, more extensive list. Wine orders may be taken and wine served by the waiter, the captain, or by a wine steward or sommelier. Whatever the procedure used, it takes effort to build good wine sales. Operations with good full-bottle wine sales not only present wine lists as a standard procedure, they also train their personnel in suggesting wines and asking for the order.

Glassware used for wine service can consist of an all-purpose glass—about 8 ounces—and a champagne glass. Champagne connoisseurs prefer the tall tulip (or flute) glass (which tapers in at the top to trap the bubbles) over the flat coupe or saucer champagne glass.

Some restaurants use a 7-ounce white wine glass and a 9-ounce red wine glass. A restaurant with an extensive wine operation may use special glassware for each type of wine, such as a large balloon glass for Burgundy, and a smaller, tall-stemmed glass with a squat, round bowl for German wines.

In the past, the service of wine has been surrounded with a lot of mystique and sometimes just plain hokum. Actually, the steps of service are quite simple and based on common sense. They are as follows:

1. Obtain the wine from either the wine cellar or the bar. If the bartender holds the stock, present either a machine-generated duplicate or a full-bottle wine slip to him. (This will be used by the bartender to get a replacement bottle for his inventory, since he will not have an empty bottle to turn in.)
2. Present the bottle to the table's host, to show him that he is getting the wine that he ordered (see fig. 6-3). Do not cover the label with a napkin. White wines are presented as soon as they are ordered, and then put into a wine cooler with ice and water. Red wines are presented with the food course with which they will be drunk (generally the entrée; sometimes the appetizer). Appropriate glassware is put on the table when the bottle is opened.
3. Open the bottle, using a "waiter's friend" lever-type or a prong-type corkscrew. Usually, the bottle is opened right at the table. However, in a very elegant operation, the bottle may be opened at a side stand or in the pantry, especially if it is very old and the cork is likely to be dry or dirty. Present the cork to the table's host.

   Some experts say that red wines should be opened ahead

6-3. The presentation of a red wine in Celler In The Sky, one of the dining rooms of Windows On The World. The Cellar In The Sky offers a prix fixe menu that includes four kinds of wine. (Photograph Ezra Stoller © Esto. Courtesy of Inhilco and Windows On The World.)

of time to allow them to "breathe." It is debatable, however, how much breathing a full bottle of wine can do, since the amount of surface exposed to the air in the neck of a bottle is very small. Wines do breathe in the glass, however, and the balloon-type red wine glass is designed to expose a large surface of liquid to the air.

4. When the bottle is opened and ready to be served, pour about one ounce into the host's glass for approval. When it is approved, pour wine to all guests and the host, filling the glasses to not more than one-half capacity. Twist the bottle slightly before lifting it away from each glass to prevent drips on the tablecloth; a napkin should be on hand to catch any drops. Replace white wine in the wine cooler.

5. During service, replenish the glasses from the bottle, and remove the bottle (and cooler, if it is a white wine) when empty. When clearing the food course, remove empty wine glasses.

7
Responsible Beverage Service
James E. Peters

The retail alcohol beverage industry is faced with one of its greatest challenges in recent years. Public outcry over drunk driving and alcohol abuse is forcing the industry to promote its most profitable item in a way which emphasizes responsible use without allowing excess.

In recent months, many owners and managers have initiated awareness programs designed to inform employees of their social and legal responsibilities. Although many walk away from these programs asking "Are we bartenders or babysitters?," most realize that they have a duty to protect their customers.

Reprinted with permission of *Restaurant Business Magazine* from the article "Are We Bartenders or Babysitters?" in their May 20, 1984 issue.

James E. Peters is executive director of the Responsible Hospitality Institute, a group based in Springfield, Massachusetts, that provides legal- and social-responsibility training programs for the hospitality industry.

Alcohol servers are often unable to recognize when someone is "legally" intoxicated, and they may not know how to control intoxicated behavior. Additional information is needed.

Intoxication may be directly controlled by a server who recognizes its symptoms and refuses service to someone who shows signs of inebriation. The server's attitude can also act indirectly to discourage excessive drinking.

Alcohol is a depressant drug; its primary effect is to slow down the nervous system. Behavioral changes are related to the concentration of alcohol in the blood, and usually follow a recognizable pattern beginning with loss of inhibition, progressing to slurred speech, loss of coordination, and aggressiveness, and culminating in loss of consciousness. Driving ability is impaired in most people with a blood alcohol concentration (BAC) of 0.10, which in most states defines legal intoxication.

BAC is determined by how much a person drinks, their weight, and the rate at which alcohol is consumed. Whether a person eats or not before or while drinking, their sex, mood, the strength of the drink, and basic physiological differences between people can also affect BAC. Alcoholics and experienced drinkers can often consume large quantities of alcohol without displaying obvious signs of intoxication. These people might not appear intoxicated with a BAC of 0.10, but their driving ability will still be impaired.

The most simple and reliable way to monitor a person's degree of intoxication is by counting drinks; only a carefully monitored breath analyzer will be more accurate. A certain number of drinks will signal that an intervention is necessary.

During an intervention, a person's behavior can be more easily changed if they are provided with positive alternatives. Showing concern for the patron will lessen the chance of confrontation.

Managing the intoxicated person requires skill, alertness, and patience; every situation is different. Role playing and reenactments of problem situations can become a regular part of staff meetings, developing greater confidence and perception among the staff. It can also be helpful to bring in a counselor or nurse from a community detoxification center or a local police officer to discuss the techniques they use when dealing with intoxicated persons.

As a server making an intervention, it is important to remain calm; one must be quiet but firm, and not become defensive. The person will often not remember the encounter the next day. What someone who is inebriated will say should not be taken personally, and a server, manager, or owner should not get into a shouting match. Keep statements simple and direct; repeating statements can help reduce the chance of an aggressive escalation. Remember that the more complex behaviors, such as judgment, learning, and reasoning, are the first to be affected by alcohol. Trying to be rational and reasonable with an intoxicated person can become quite frustrating.

Be assertive, and deal with issues at hand; do not let the person sidetrack you. Making a statement such as "I am concerned about you and want to be sure you get home safely" is much less threatening than "You have had too much; you are drunk and cannot drive."

A server must always be prepared to deal with aggression. An intervention must be handled carefully in order not to escalate the encounter. Try to distract the person from the source of anger, but beware of statements that can be misinterpreted, such as "Let's step outside and talk about this." Shifting the focus of responsibility can help reduce tension. "It's the law," or "house policy," or "I'll lose my job," will make you seem less threatening. Do not touch the person without a prior explanation; if a person attacks you, use only enough force to restrain the person. If you need help, get it! Establishing a positive, open relationship with local law enforcement agencies is extremely important. If they are aware of your standard operating procedures and know you only call them in emergencies, they will respond appropriately.

A confrontive situation can be avoided by offering positive alternatives. Inviting someone to your establishment, letting them drink until they are intoxicated, and then asking them to leave is not only irresponsible, but bad business.

Encourage people to try alternative nonalcoholic beverages. Appealing, profitable "mocktails" are successfully sold by many operators, and there are also many nonalcoholic and low-alcoholic types of beer and wine available. Lounge menus, tent cards, and chalkboards are all being used to promote these beverages. The health-conscious, responsible drinking public is becoming tired of "club soda with a twist of lime" as their only alternative. Be creative and imaginative. Fifty-five million American adults do not drink alcoholic beverages at all.

An increasing number of restaurants and taverns are keeping their kitchens open later in the evening. The public has become more aware of drinking and driving, and people are choosing to order a late-night snack rather than a last drink "for the road." Encouraging your customers to stay later for something to eat will allow the one cure for intoxication to work—time.

Try to encourage intoxicated customers to take a cab or go home with a friend. Free ride services supported by local drinking establishments or community groups are available in many communities. Reasonable care must be exercised in preventing a customer from driving. Wrestling with them in the parking lot to get their keys or tying them to a chair is not only dangerous, but can lead to a lawsuit for violation of civil rights and false imprisonment. Letting the air out of the tires or calling the police are safer alternatives for the customer and for others on the road.

The most important strategy in controlling intoxication is preventing it from happening. Some studies have shown an establishment's decor and environment to be directly related to the number of aggressive acts and incidents of intoxication. Jim Schaefer of the University of Minnesota has discussed how controlling such factors as lighting, music, dance floor space, and decor can reduce intoxicated behavior.

Table arrangements, seating, and capacity are other factors to consider. Placing tables and seats to allow a free flow of traffic and good supervision of all areas is a way to reduce risk. Limiting the number of people in a room will reduce crowding and anxiety in customers. Being "three deep at the bar and not able to get a drink" does not increase sales; it only prevents courteous and efficient service.

For example, one restaurant in a large college community had the most popular "happy hour" in town. But, after a dram shop lawsuit, some of their policies were changed. The number of people in the lounge was limited, and a "two-fer" munchie menu with a variety of bar foods was created. Lounge sales soon began to drop off, but a change in clientele was noticed. The customers in the lounge began to stay later than the happy hour, and dinner sales began to increase. Old customers returned, pleased they were again able to get a parking space previously taken by the "happy hour" crowd. An alternative beverage menu was designed, and the staff was trained to recognize intoxicated behavior and to refuse service. Management supported the judgment of the staff, and alternative transportation was offered when necessary.

Their income statements began to show a reduction in costs for the replacement of glassware, repair of furniture, vandalized bathrooms and walls, and general maintenance. Although lounge sales were reduced, beverage sales in the dining room offset the losses.

Finding and keeping lounge service staff had always been a problem. Now there is a waiting list. A more controlled drinking environment allows staff to pay more attention to customers, thereby increasing tips and creating a more enjoyable workplace.

Controlling intoxication is a challenge the retail alcohol beverage industry must meet if it is to continue to maintain the respect of the public. Training staff to recognize intoxication and to intervene in a nonconfrontive manner is one alternative, but preventing intoxication by creating a safe, responsible drinking environment is clearly the most sensible and cost-effective solution.

8

Dining Room Operation

Thus far the focus in the book has been on technical aspects of service. This chapter deals with the administrative side of running a dining room and includes information on maintaining the premises, assigning stations, holding lineups to brief the staff, seating guests, assigning sidework, and record keeping (scheduling the staff, preparing payroll information, and controlling costs).

DINING ROOM INSPECTION

The appearance and condition of the dining room should be checked before each meal. The dining room supervisor should allow enough time to make this inspection and correct any unacceptable conditions before the dining room opens. Problems with air conditioning, heating, or ventilation should be referred to the manager or maintenance department for immediate action. Some last minute cleaning or replenishing of supplies and wares may be required. The supervisor should also be alert to potential safety hazards and correct them immediately.

Some companies use a checklist for this purpose. This helps anyone substituting in the job. The checklist provides a written plan for that specific dining room. Checklists will vary depending on the type of operation, equipment, and architectural details in the room. The major items to be checked in most foodservice operations are as follows:

- Doors
- Cashier's station
- Floors and carpets
- Walls
- Table settings
- Ashtrays, sugar bowls, salt and pepper shakers
- Menus
- Lamps and lamp shades
- Windows
- Curtains, shades, and draperies
- Mirrors and pictures
- Table linen
- Chairs (including reserve high chairs)
- Condiment containers
- Table legs (for steadiness)
- Tablecloths (for even hanging)
- Table legs and chair legs (for splinters)
- Side stands and supplies

The room's light, heat, and ventilation should also be checked.

The inspection should not be limited to the inside of the building. Many restaurants have dining rooms or lobbies that are visible from the street. The view presented to pedestrians can be a strong selling tool or a total turnoff. Dead bugs and dust on the windowsill tell potential guests something about the cleanliness of the kitchen. A view of an attractively set up dining room may entice the passerby to come back for dinner, but messy-looking tables with last night's soiled tablecloths will not appeal.

ASSIGNING STATIONS

The seats and tables assigned to each waiter or team of waiters are called a *station*. The number of tables assigned will depend on the number of seats, the frequency of their turnover, the competence of the particular waiter, the distance to the kitchen, and the number of waiters scheduled for the particular meal. At a fast-turnover counter operation, a waiter may only be able to handle six or seven seats even though the distance to the pickup areas may be only a few feet. On the other hand, in a dining room with only a moderate turnover and an even flow of patrons, a waiter may be able to serve as many as sixteen to twenty seats (see figs. 8-1 and 8-2).

In some dining rooms, stations are fixed and permanently assigned to each waiter. A relief waiter, usually one with little seniority, relieves each station on that waiter's day off. The fixed-station system is usually unfair to younger members of the staff because they are limited to the less desirable stations. Once this system is in practice, however, it is very difficult to change.

A more flexible and equitable arrangement is to rotate stations and vary the station size according to the volume of business expected and the number of waiters scheduled. Every dining room has some seats and stations that are more desirable to the guests than others, and it is quite impractical to try to force the guests onto the less desirable stations when more attractive seats are available. Although stations can be planned to balance some of the workload, the rotation of stations among the staff is a more equitable way of balancing the work.

When a lower volume of business is forecast and the dining room is not staffed to capacity, station assignments can be enlarged. In this way, the entire room is assigned even though the number of waiters is reduced. Sections of the room can be closed off, depending on the architectural plan of the room and the expected flow of business. In slower periods a smaller room

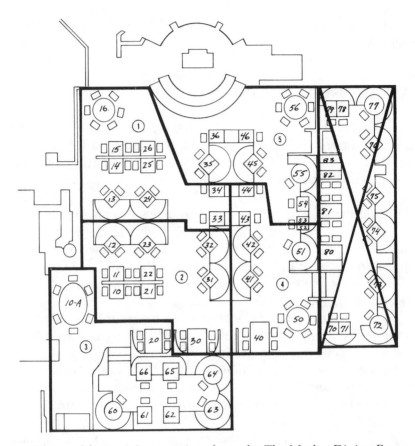

8-1. This and figure 8-2 are station charts for The Market Dining Room in the World Trade Center, New York. This shows the stations when five teams of waiters are scheduled. (Courtesy of The Market Dining Rooms and Bar and Inhilco.)

that is kept full provides a better image and atmosphere than a large room that is a sea of tablecloths (see figs. 8-1 and 8-2).

LINEUPS

Lineups are short dining room staff meetings at which the staff is inspected for neatness of dress and personal cleanliness. Station assignments are usually made at that time, and the service

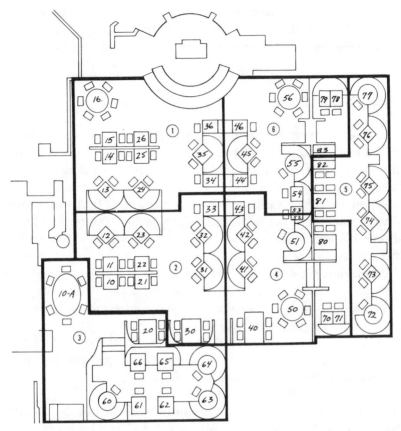

8-2. This shows the stations from figure 8-1 when six teams of waiters are used. (Courtesy of The Market Dining Rooms and Bar and Inhilco.)

staff is briefed on the menu for the day. This briefing should include the following:

1. The prices of all menu items, their contents, and the method of preparation.
2. A discussion of made-to-order items.
3. The location in the kitchen where an item is to be found.
4. The approximate time required to wait for items prepared to order.
5. The items that should be promoted and any planned substitutes in the event of runouts.

6. The tasting of new dishes and instruction for their service.

7. A review of the correct service of other menu items.

8. A discussion of any guest complaints pertaining to service.

SEATING

When seating guests, the host must consider any special needs or requests of the guest, the status of service on each station at that moment, and the number of guests each station already has.

When seating a guest with a special need, that need must always come first. For instance, a guest who is disabled or feeble should be seated close to the door so he will not have to navigate through a dining room full of furniture. A family with small children needs a quiet table off to the side where the youngsters will not bother other guests. A television personality or local politician may want to sit at center stage where he can see and be seen, or he may want privacy.

Most guests do not need that kind of special consideration. They just want a good table where they can get good service. Unless another table is clearly preferable to the one assigned to them, they will accept the assigned table. If arriving guests are seated in each station in rotation, each waiter can devote his attention to each of his tables in turn. Furthermore, each waiter will receive about the same number of guests and will, therefore, have a fairly equal share of the workload and the tips. Unfortunately, it does not always work that smoothly, and the host should always be aware of the status of service on a station before he seats another party there. If the waiter is stuck (unable to deliver the desired level of service for any reason), giving him more people will only make him more stuck and further delay service to the guests he already has. *Seating must always be in consideration of the guest and not the staff.*

Electronic table management systems are now available that keep track of the status of every table in the dining room. These systems are especially effective in large, high-volume operations. The ability to reseat vacated tables quickly has a definite impact on sales.

A display screen from one such system is shown in figure 8-3. Tables are shown by table number (the number on top); below the table number are the number of seats at the table, the station numbers, and the status of the table. In the example, all tables are O, or occupied. The bottom line of the figure displays the prompts for changing the status of a table (seat, clear, block), and for displaying the guest list by table number, the waiting list, and the reservation list. At the end of the day (EOD), productivity data is produced. A light pen is used to change the configuration of tables if they are rearranged.

Although the host should try to give each waiter an equal chance to make his tips, in every crew there are one or more waiters who are able to handle more covers than the others. These more productive workers should not be penalized.

When guests seat themselves, a more flexible station assignment is needed to spread the workload and the tips and to give

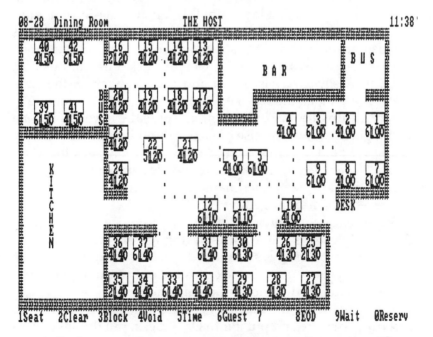

8-3. A display screen from a computerized reservation system. (Courtesy of PC Systems Inc. and Mega Computer Systems.)

the best service to all guests. One way to accomplish this is to assign fewer seats to a station that is more popular than others. Another way is to have waiters work in teams, covering sections of the room rather than individual stations. Tips may be shared by the entire crew by pooling.

CONTROLLING BREAKAGE AND LINEN COSTS

Although much of the china and glassware breakage takes place in the dishroom, it may not all be the fault of the dishroom personnel. Badly stacked trays and poor sorting of ware by waiters and busboys can be the cause of a breakage problem. Mishandling of linen can also cause stained, worn tablecloths and napkins. If linens are allowed to get wet with water or wine, the fabric can rot or be permanently stained before it is processed by the laundry.

The staff should also be trained to use care in emptying ashtrays. A live ash or smoldering butt is a potential source of fires. The National Fire Protection Association ranks cigarette sparks in trash or linen hampers as a major cause of restaurant fires.

There is a right and a wrong way to stack a tray or bus box. On a tray, silverware is sorted and laid together on the side. Plates are scraped and stacked in order of size in the middle of the tray. Cups are stacked around the outside, never more than two high. Glassware is also placed around the rim of the tray. Glasses should never be stacked since they may stick together. Paper placemats and napkins are wadded up and put on top. If table linen is used, linen napkins are tucked under the arm to prevent them from getting wet (see fig. 8-4).

Bus boxes are usually used only in fast-service dining rooms; the principles of sorting and stacking are the same as when trays are used. Busboys should be trained not to dump a whole table full of ware into a bus box. It is not only hard on the ware, it is also hard on the guests' ears and nerves.

In the dishroom the busboy or waiter is usually required to sort the glassware and put it into glass racks, put the silverware into a soak pan or sink, and put the linen into a linen hamper. Sometimes he is required to stack the plates by size on the dish

8-4. Loading of a hotel oval tray. The heaviest weights (stacked plates, silver, and coffeepot) are over the shoulder or arm. Glasses and cups are around the edge of the tray and linen is tucked under the arm. If paper placemats and napkins are used, they are wadded up on top of the tray.

table. Whether or not he does this will depend on the size of the operation and the number of dishroom personnel.

Linen cost control involves correct use of clean linen as well as preventing damage to soiled linen. The use of napkins as side towels or for cleaning should be strictly forbidden. Another source of unnecessary cost is the use of cloths that are larger than needed for the table. General carelessness in handling of clean linens is another source of loss. Commercial laundries will usually give credit for linens that are unuseable because of stains, tears, or holes. The staff should be trained to put such linens aside for credit.

The dining room supervisor's responsibility for his staff's performance does not end at the kitchen door. He must train his people to handle linen and ware properly and to follow through on supervision. In this area, he will need to work with the executive steward or back-of-the-house manager.

SIDEWORK

Sidework is the name given to the dining room housekeeping jobs usually performed by the service staff. Since time spent in this work does not produce tips directly, some waiters object to doing it. Unfortunately, they do not realize that poor housekeeping affects the appearance of the room, the efficiency of service, and future sales. Typical sidework jobs include cleaning the salt and pepper shakers and sugar bowls; care of condiments and containers; polishing silver; dusting, straightening, and replenishing side stands; care of flowers or plants; polishing tabletops; and care of decorative items in the room (see fig. 8-5.)

These jobs may be scheduled daily or weekly and should be specifically assigned on a rotating basis. Posting a weekly schedule of sidework assignments usually eliminates any misunderstandings. Written instructions for each task should be posted so everyone understands what is involved in each job (see fig. 8-6).

A sample description of station closing duties for a coffee shop operation follows.[1]

Replenish Salt, Pepper, Sugar, and Condiments

Carry shakers, sugar bowls, and condiments on a cocktail tray to the far corner and do the work there. Do *not* do at stations in front of customers.

1. Refill salt and pepper shakers and sugar bowls to the very top. Refill over cocktail tray to avoid spills onto floor. Clean tops, sides, and bottoms of shakers and sugar bowls.
2. Marry catsups and mustards. Do not fill to the very top—only to the manufacturer's full level. Completely clean all condiment

[1]Used by permission of Inhilco, One World Trade Center, New York, New York.

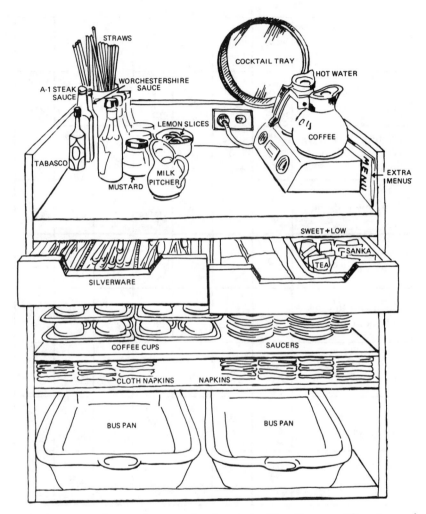

8-5. Correct side stand setup for lunch in The Corner. (Courtesy of The Corner and Inhilco.)

bottles, inside and outside of bottle necks, and inside and outside of bottle caps. Do this with a damp rag—do not get water in the bottles. If necessary, get additional condiments from the storeroom to replenish each station with:

- Four catsups (full bottles)
- Two mustards (full bottles)
- One Worcestershire sauce
- One Tabasco

	Sun	Mon	Tues	Wed	Thur	Fri	Sat
Salts, Peppers, and Sugar Bowls	Mary	Steve	Sheila	Sal	Maria	Willie	Charley
Dusting Woodwork, Window Sills, and Railings	Linda	Mary	Steve	Jose	Sheila	Paul	Willie
Condiment Bottles	Paul	Willie	Mary	Steve	Jose	Sal	Maria
Clean and Restock Sidestand #1	Maria	Paul	Ruth	Mary	Steve	Jose	Sal
Clean and Restock Sidestand #2	X CLOSED	X CLOSED	Sal	Sheila	Charley	Linda	X CLOSED
Wash High Chairs and Booster Seats	Willie	Linda	Paul	Charley	Mary	Steve	Jose
Dining Room Refrigator	Sheila	Ruth	Jose	Maria	Willie	Charley	Linda
Flowers	Ruth	Sheila	Charley	Ruth	Sal	Maria	Paul

8-6. Sidework assignments.

Clean Station

1. Wipe all exposed shelf surfaces.
2. Clean coffee warmer—top, sides, and bottom—and shelf underneath it.

Restock

- Lunch napkins (leave two bundles of folded linen per station)
- Sanka

- Tea
- Sugar substitute
- Jam packets (grape, orange, and strawberry)
- Cocktail tray on every station

You should always leave a station in the same condition in which you found it—fully stocked and clean. If the station is closing for the day, do the following:

Clean Counters/Tables

1. Strip completely bare.
2. Clean top and edges.
3. Clean four inches into bottom of tables.
4. Remove all items from side stand counter, clean thoroughly, and set up again.

Reset Counters/Tables

1. Place clean ashtray, shakers, and sugar bowls on counter/table. Use one setup per table or per every two counter seats.
2. Set for next day. Place cups face down.

Store Perishable Items

1. Whenever possible, marry cream and milk, juices, lemon slices, and fruit salad into stations that are still open.
2. If not possible, tightly cover lemon slices with plastic wrap and put in island refrigerator.
3. Always refill juice pitchers (two orange, one grapefruit, and one tomato), tightly cover with plastic wrap, and store in island refrigerator. Discard any remaining cream and milk in pitchers. Use clean pitchers every night.
4. Give remaining cake and fruit salad to the kitchen.

Miscellaneous

1. Unplug coffee warmers. Wash pots and fill halfway with water.
2. Arrange shelves underneath the counters.

Fridays Only

1. Empty salt, pepper, and sugar into pitchers. Cover with plastic wrap and label. Put shakers and sugar bowls into bus pans for washing. Do not do this in front of customers.
2. Wash coffeepots in the dishwasher.
3. Store unopened dairy containers and whole lemons in the walk-in.
4. Discard opened dairy containers, any remaining juice in pitchers, lemon slices, and cake.

DINING ROOM RECORD KEEPING

The dining room supervisor does not usually have much paperwork, but he has several important clerical tasks.

Staff Schedules and Payroll Records

Schedules should be posted well in advance so workers can make their personal plans. Accurate records of time worked must be kept. Scheduling and payroll record keeping are discussed in chapter 16.

Cover Counts

As guests are seated, the maître d' or seating host records the number of guests assigned to each waiter or station. At the close of the meal, these counts are totaled. They provide a means of measuring each waiter's productivity. The total count is also a control tool. It is compared to the cashier's count for the meal to determine that payment was collected from each guest seated. If there is a discrepancy, the cashier can then compare the counts by waiter or station to determine who is responsible.

Dining Room Logbook

The supervisor's logbook is a very important record of daily department activity. This log should be a bound book with at least one page for each day. In chapter 4, the use of the logbook for recording guest comments and complaints was discussed. This book can also be a very important record of daily department activity. In addition to logging guest complaints and how they were handled, the supervisor on each shift should record all pertinent information about the day's business: the weather, cover counts, special parties, accidents, personnel matters, maintenance requests, and so forth. This provides a means of communicating current activity and pending matters to supervisors on other shifts, as well as forming a permanent record of the room's activity. This record could also be invaluable in cases of insurance liability claims or personnel matters.

Other Types of Paperwork

These may include accident reports, employee disciplinary warnings, hiring requests, and employment terminations. All are discussed in later chapters.

LEGAL ASPECTS OF DINING ROOM OPERATION

Government has been playing a larger role in the day-to-day operation of all businesses. Here is a sampling of the types of legislation affecting restaurants.

Federal

- OSHA—The Williams-Steiger Occupational Safety and Health Act of 1970
- Equal Employment Opportunity Commission regulations pertaining to equal employment opportunity legislation
- National Labor Relations Act
- Fair Employment Practices laws, including the Age Discrimination in Employment Act
- Federal Wage and Hour Law
- The Privacy Act of 1974
- IRS tip-reporting requirements
- The Immigration Reform and Control Act of 1986

State and Local

- Alcoholic beverage control regulations (liquor laws)
- Department of health or sanitation regulations
- Fire department and occupancy codes
- Consumer protection legislation, such as antismoking and truth-in-menu laws
- State wage and hour laws

Safety

Federal law requires that a safe working environment be provided for employees; common sense demands that safe premises be maintained for everyone who enters. The National Restaurant Association (311 First Street, N.W., Washington DC 20001) publishes the *Safety Self-Inspection Program for Food Service Operators*, a handy guide for checking on OSHA compliance and safe conditions for the public.

Most accidents in public areas employing dining room personnel involve falls and strains caused by improper lifting. Falls are often the result of wet floors, debris on the floor, obstacles in main traffic aisles, and loose or torn carpets. These areas should be included in the supervisor's inspection checklist. However, surveillance should not be limited to the preopening inspection. A potential hazard may develop at any time and must be removed at once.

Fire Safety

Fire safety ordinances have come a long way since the disastrous Cocoanut Grove fire in 1942 took 491 lives; yet in June 1977, 160 people died and more than 100 were injured in a Kentucky supper club fire. More recently, 96 people died on December 31, 1986 in a Puerto Rico hotel casino fire. Although fire codes come under the jurisdiction of local governments, the Occupational Safety and Health Administration (OSHA) developed a fire protection checklist for hotels and motels. It is also useful for restaurant operators, and is reproduced below.

1. Emergency plan developed and discussed with employees?
2. Emergency drills conducted at least annually?

3. Employee emergency alarms distinctive, operating properly?
4. Smoke detectors, alarms in good working order?
5. Water sprinkler systems in good condition?
6. All exits clearly marked and unobstructed?
7. All exits and exit signs appropriately illuminated?
8. Sufficient exit capacity available for occupancy?
9. Stairways in good condition with appropriate railings?
10. Fire doors installed as required and in proper operating condition?
11. Fire walls located as required?
12. Flammable materials stored in proper containers?
13. "No Smoking" areas clearly marked?
14. Portable fire extinguisher readily accessible, inspected monthly, recharged regularly?
15. Employees taught to use extinguisher?
16. Local fire department aware of hotel facilities and fire protection systems?

EEOC and Other Federal Regulations

EEOC and the other federal regulations listed have to do mostly with employment and hiring practices. They are discussed in chapter 13.

However, in addition to its implication for hiring practices, the Civil Rights Act of 1964 is also the basis for sexual harassment prohibitions. The Equal Employment Opportunity Commission considers unwelcome sexual advances and requests for sexual favors or other sexually-related behavior, including verbal behavior, to be discriminatory and illegal, if a condition of a worker's employment is submission to such conduct, or if such conduct substantially interferes with the worker's job performance, or if it creates an intimidating, hostile, or offensive working environment. Sexual harassment can involve not only supervisors, but also coworkers and customers. Charges have been filed against restaurant owners and managers in cases where managers knew (or should have known) about harassing behavior by coworkers or customers and took no action to stop it. In a number of cases involving harassment of waitresses by guests, the issue centered around a requirement that the women wear revealing costumes.

The law applies equally to both sexes; male employees have filed sexual harassment charges, too.

The Age Discrimination in Employment Act and its amendment protects workers between the ages of forty and seventy from arbitrary discrimination based on age, including hiring, firing, pay, promotions, fringe benefits, and other work-related concerns. This law has an extra set of teeth in that workers winning an age discrimination case are awarded double the amount of their damages—lost wages plus costs.

The National Labor Relations Act pertains to union-management relations and union organizing activities. This is discussed in chapter 15.

The Immigration Reform and Control Act requires that organizations verify that a job applicant is not an unauthorized alien before he can be hired. The law provides penalties for hiring illegal aliens.

Liquor Laws

A liquor license is one of the most valuable assets a restaurant can have. Loss of that license due to a violation of local liquor laws can be very costly. Typical violations include serving alcoholic beverages to minors or obviously intoxicated patrons, serving after legal hours, or employing individuals who are prohibited from working in licensed operations under the law. The dining room manager should have an up-to-date copy of those local alcoholic beverage regulations that pertain to the operation's particular type of license, and should know those regulations thoroughly.

Even more costly these days than a loss of license is third-party liability. Chapter 7 deals with this important issue.

Sanitation

We tend to think of sanitation and health inspections as involving only the back of the house. However, they affect the front of the house as well. It is the front that the guest sees.

He must draw his conclusions about the cleanliness of the kitchen and the safety of the food from the conditions and practices he sees in the dining rooms and public areas of the establishment, especially the rest rooms.

Areas of primary concern to the dining room manager are personal cleanliness of the staff, including clothing and bodily cleanliness, use of hair nets or caps, and absence of communicable diseases; food and equipment handling practices, such as the use of tongs, forks, and spoons to dish up food; handling sanitized silverware by the handles and not by the eating ends; proper handling of ice to prevent contamination; proper storage of food used by the dining room staff, such as sugar and other condiments; cleanliness of rest room facilities; and general housekeeping. If there are any refrigeration units in the dining area, they must be maintained at the proper temperatures.

The National Restaurant Association (311 First Street N.W., Washington DC 20001) publishes a *Self-Inspection Program for Food Service Operators on Sanitation and Safe Food Handling.* It is a handy management tool for setting sanitation standards and for checking performance.

Consumer Protection Legislation

Three types of consumer protection legislation directly affect restaurant service operations. They are:

- Truth-in-menu regulations.
- Maintenance of nonsmoking areas.
- Requirements for the posting of signs pertaining to the Heimlich maneuver (for assisting a choking victim) and warnings to pregnant women on the use of liquor.

At this time, these types of legislation do exist in some areas. (Whether or not the antismoking supporters will gain wide support is hard to say.) The actual effectiveness of posting signs, however, is also debatable.

Truth-in-menu should be standard operating procedure for any business, regardless of whether it is required by law. It makes no sense to falsely promote an item. Saying that fish is fresh when it is frozen or that meat is prime when it is not only raises false expectations in the guest. Unfulfilled expectations cause guest dissatisfaction. Furthermore, some restaurants that falsely claimed to be serving branded food products have been sued by the manufacturers, who have become quite protective of their trademarks.

Truth-in-menu legislation generally deals with the following types of misrepresentations:

1. The point of origin of the product is not as advertised.
2. The size, weight, or portion is not as advertised.
3. The quality or grade of the product is not as advertised.
4. The product is adulterated in one of the following ways:

   - A valuable constituent has been omitted from the product, either in whole or in part.
   - A substance is used to replace the product, either in whole or in part.
   - The product is damaged or inferior, and this fact has been concealed.
   - A substance (other than seasoning) has been added or mixed so as to increase the weight, diminish the quality, or make the product appear better than it is.

Thus, "Fresh Shrimp Cocktail" is probably a violation of truth-in-menu laws, since virtually all shrimp is marketed frozen; "Roquefort Dressing" had better be made with Roquefort cheese; and "Coke" had better be the Coca-Cola product. "Idaho Baked Potato" must come from Idaho and "Whipped Cream" had better be the real thing.

Truth-in-menu is not limited to what is printed on the menu card; it also applies to oral representations made by the dining room staff.

CIVIL LAW SUITS

It is said that the American public is more apt to sue than any other population in the world. Anyone can file a lawsuit against another person or against a business or organization for any cause, and the party sued must then be prepared to defend itself against the suit. The best defense is to minimize the chance of being sued by striving to ensure that no one is wronged or injured. The next best defense is to keep very careful records of incidents that might result in a lawsuit. One critical issue facing the restaurant industry at this time is that of third-party liability for accidents caused by drunken drivers. This is discussed in chapter 7.

Prevention of accidents that could lead to lawsuits and negligence claims is part of the supervisor's job. Another type of claim is for physical assault or verbal abuse by an employee or another person. The courts have held that a restaurant keeper has a duty to provide protection to his patrons from insult or annoyance while they are in his restaurant. To put a stop to such annoyance, he may eject the person guilty of the offense. As for protection from assaults, the courts have required that all reasonable care be taken to prevent such assaults. Certainly this includes careful screening of employees hired to work in contact with the public. Any employee who cannot curb either his fists or his tongue should not be permitted to work in a dining room.

Dealing with a guest you suspect of stealing is very touchy. Do not make accusations. Raise questions until you are absolutely sure and have proof to press charges.

In any case, whether it be an accident or other type of incident, be sure you record all the details in your logbook. Be very specific as to who was involved, who said what to whom, when and where it happened, and what conditions existed at the time. Such a record could be invaluable in the event of a lawsuit.

9

Merchandising and Sales Promotion

Developing an overall merchandising and sales program for a restaurant is the responsibility of management. Because the dining room manager is in daily contact with the customers, his suggestions will probably be sought on those aspects of merchandising related to dining room operations.

Once the merchandising program is developed, the dining room manager is responsible for carrying out his part of the program. This may include training the staff in salesmanship, special service techniques, internal advertising materials and point of sales displays, and promotional giveaways.

Selling and service techniques were discussed briefly in chapter 4 as part of the standards of service. They must be incorporated into the steps of service.

SALESMANSHIP

The professional waiter and waitress are not just order takers and carriers of trays. First and foremost, they must be salespersons. Their function is not only to get the customer served today, but also to get that customer to return again . . . and again. While that guest is in the restaurant, the salesman-waiter can suggest items that will increase the guest's enjoyment of his meal, increase the restaurant's sales, and increase the waiter's tips.

The first rule of salesmanship is *know your product*. In a restaurant this means that the service staff must know the menu items, as well as the major ingredients and the methods of preparation. If wines are sold, the staff should know the wine list thoroughly (see fig. 9-1). Most important, they should know what the food items and wines taste like. It is difficult to be an enthusiastic salesman for something you have never tasted. The cost of food and wines used for periodic tasting and training sessions is a small investment that should produce large returns. (Incidentally, the service staff is often a good taste panel for evaluating new recipes.)

The second rule of selling is *know your customer*. If at all possible, know his name and address him by it. That is basic human relations. In restaurants where customers make reservations, the guest identifies himself when he arrives. From then on, it should be easy for the staff to continue addressing him by name. The maître d' or seating host can copy the guest's name onto a small piece of paper, along with the number of the assigned table. When he seats the party, he discreetly gives the slip to the captain or waiter. In hotel dining rooms, conference guests and conventioneers make the task easy by wearing badges or name tags. Some discretion is necessary, however, if the name tags give only first names. Not everyone likes to be addressed familiarly by people they do not know.

In informal, fast-turnover restaurants, it becomes a bit more difficult to learn guests' names, but it still can be done. The host certainly should know who his regular customers are, and he can pass their names along to the waiter or waitress serving them.

9-1. Merchandising wines at Cellar In The Sky. (Photograph © Ezra Stoller. Courtesy of Inhilco and Windows On The World.)

However, salesmanship goes beyond knowing the customer's name. It includes knowing his tastes and preferences. In a restaurant with a large amount of repeat business from a regular clientele, the staff usually learns the tastes and preferences of the regulars. Where there is a large transient clientele, it becomes more difficult but not impossible. An observant waiter who pays attention to his guests can learn a great deal about their tastes and preferences by the things they order and the way they order. This does not involve prying or eavesdropping, just paying attention to what the guests are saying when they give their orders.

The self-assured guest who knows exactly what he wants and orders a complete meal without any suggestion from the waiter needs no selling; he has already sold himself. The waiter-salesman then concentrates on providing the best service to sell this guest on coming back again. The guest who hesitates or asks questions will appreciate suggestions from the waiter. Some may just want to be reassured that the item they have selected is a good choice. Others want to be guided in their selection. These guests are most likely to make impulse sales if positive suggestive selling techniques are used.

The third rule of selling is *match the product to the customer's needs or preferences.* True salesmanship is not just hard selling to push volume sales. Rather, it is matching what you have to sell with what the customer wants to buy. In the restaurant, the waiter-salesman must match his menu to the customer's tastes and preferences and then make selling suggestions that will get a positive response. A steak-and-potatoes guest may be receptive to a suggestion of shrimp cocktail or apple pie à la mode. A guest who is dieting will not appreciate being tempted with a hot fudge sundae or a rich pastry, though he may be very receptive to a dish of fresh strawberries or melon for dessert. The high-protein dieter could be interested in a selection of cheeses instead of a dessert. For the anniversary couple, you may suggest a bottle of champagne; and for the executive with an expense account, a cognac after dinner and a good cigar.

Salesmanship is not limited to the more elegant restaurants. In moderately priced coffee shops, selling suggestions by the service staff can increase sales of first courses and desserts as well as side orders such as salads, french fries, and large size drinks.

The fourth rule of selling is *don't promote it if you can't produce it.* In dining room selling, this means that the service staff must have up-to-the-minute information about the availability of each menu item and know which items are running low.

Along the same line is a corollary rule: *give good service.* People expect good service when they go out to eat. If expectations are built up for a great meal, great service, and a great experience, the letdown will be twice as great if these things fail to materialize.

The fifth rule of selling is *be positive and enthusiastic.* How many desserts do you think have been sold with this line: "You don't want any dessert, do you?" Not many. "Any dessert here?" is not much better. Preferable is: "Are you folks ready for dessert? We have some terrific strawberry whipped cream pie tonight." When the guest asks, "How's the seafood plate?" he is fishing for reassurance. A lukewarm response such as "It's OK" does nothing for him or for the average check. Instead: "It's very good, but we have an excellent fried fish combination plate on the complete dinner. You get soup, dessert, and our special house salad with it." An item should never be run down; another one should simply be suggested.

The sixth rule of selling is *say thank you.* By showing appreciation for his business, the waiter is recognizing that the guest is doing him a favor rather than the other way around. By showing the guest that his patronage is valued, the waiter, and, of course, the restaurant are much more likely to get his business in the future.

The last rule of selling is *know when to quit.* If the guest is not receptive this time, he may be next time. If the waiter pushes too hard, he may not get a next time.

SERVICE TECHNIQUES

An eye-catching presentation of a specialty menu item can increase impulse sales of that item and create an image and reputation for the restaurant. The item need not be exotic, but it should be profitable.

For many years The Pump Room in Chicago was one of the most famous restaurants in the country. Part of its fame was built on showmanship in the dining room. Food was carried with a flourish into the room on flaming swords, and coffee was served by a coffee boy costumed in oriental dress and feathered turban.

In another famous Chicago restaurant, Don Roth's Black-hawk, the salad was dressed at tableside in spinning salad bowls. The technique was very simple—a round metal bowl was set in a bed of crushed ice. It was the waiter's recitation, as he spun the bowl and mixed the salad, that made the show.

Showmanship is not limited to luxury restaurants. Moderately priced steak houses create a show with salad displays and sizzle platters, which give the service sound appeal as well as visual appeal. Other techniques include carving wagons, dessert carts, salad buffets, cordial wagons, and specialty servers for rolls, relishes, or other side items.

Maintaining the Image

The dining room manager does not usually make the final decisions as to what the presentation items will be. However, he is responsible for carrying out the service. If the menu items are changed frequently, he must check with the chef to find out which items are to be featured and how they are to be presented (portions, garnitures, and so forth).

It is the manager's responsibility to see that the presentation is maintained, that the service personnel do not become stale or sloppy in their presentation, that the dessert cart and salad bar are kept supplied and immaculate, that carving wagons are kept neat, orderly, and hot, that specialty servers do not neglect any tables, and that cordials are presented at the right time and with glassware sparkling. Any presentation that is not maintained from first party to last can turn off the guests, not tempt them.

Another aspect of merchandising is garniture and food presentation. In many restaurants the servers must add the garnishes to the food and drinks they serve. They may have to dish up some of the items as well. Proper plating and garnishing are part of the merchandising program. A tired, limp sprig of parsley plopped on a plate does nothing to enhance the appeal of the dish. People eat with their eyes. If the food is presented in a messy or casual way, the appeal is lost.

Sometimes a presentation is strictly for display, such as an exhibit of wines. This kind of display must also be maintained to keep its appeal fresh. It is amazing how quickly the dust can gather and take the sheen off the most attractive display. A dusty wine glass sells no wine!

INTERNAL ADVERTISING MATERIALS

The most important piece of internal promotional material in the restaurant is the menu. Usually a great deal of planning and thought go into the layout and printing of a menu to make it an effective selling tool. The dining room manager may or may not have participated in the planning process, but he definitely is responsible for the upkeep and appearance of menus presented to guests.

No self-respecting salesman would present a soiled, dog-eared piece of sales literature to a prospective customer; neither should the restaurant sales staff. Dirty, torn menus imply a dirty, sloppily run business and negate all the effort that has gone into building the public image of the restaurant. The negative effects of old, damaged menus outweigh the few pennies saved on menu printing.

Equally self-defeating is the negative effect of menus with price increases penciled in. The customer is immediately confronted with the fact that he is going to get less for his money. The small cost of printing new menus when prices must be increased is an unavoidable business expense.

Guests sometimes ask for a menu to take home. Unless the menu is printed in gold on platinum, give it to them. It is the best (and usually the cheapest) kind of advertising a restaurant can have. If the menus are very expensive, have some less expensive souvenir menus printed to give away, and be sure the name of the restaurant, the full address, and the telephone number are prominently shown.

Operators who give out souvenir menus usually have them printed without prices. In that way, a larger printing can be ordered to reduce the cost per menu. It also solves the negative image problem when raising prices.

POS—POINT-OF-SALE PROMOTION

Some restaurant operators are borrowing a technique from retailers and using POS promotional material, such as table tents, signs, posters, streamers or banners, menu clip-ons, placemats, and hats or buttons for the staff—all carrying some special promotional theme or message. The purpose is to produce an extra sale from the customer once he is in the store. In the restaurant, the promotion may be aimed at an additional sale or at switching the guest from a standard, low-profit item to a featured high-profit item.

Here again, it is the dining room manager's responsibility to see that the promotional program is carried out—that buttons are worn, that table tents are put out on every table, and that posters are displayed. Where the promotion is primarily in-house (as opposed to external advertising), the success of the promotion depends primarily on the dining room manager. He is in an excellent position to make a strong impact on sales; and his staff is in a good position to benefit from increased tips. Thus special promotions benefit employees as well as the restaurant owner.

PREMIUMS AND GIVEAWAYS

Some special promotions include giving away premiums with the purchase of a particular item. The giveaway may be glassware, coffee mugs, or teapots. This type of promotion is usually limited to fast turnover, high-volume operations, although specialty cocktail lounges may use premiums occasionally. Generally, however, they are used only in highly competitive situations because they create problems of maintaining inventories. Giveaways can also be costly and can interfere with the flow of service.

Another type of giveaway is used by higher-priced restaurants; some small favor, usually in keeping with the theme of the restaurant, is given to all guests during the course of the service. Here again the presentation must be built into the steps of service, and the dining room manager must control the supply of these items.

Family-type restaurants often have small favors for children— a special comic book about the restaurant, a menu that becomes a hat to take home, a placemat to crayon, or a treasure chest of inexpensive toys from which the child can choose.

Premiums for adults may include small flowers or leis for the ladies and cigars for the men. A western theme restaurant presents chocolate candies wrapped as gold coins; a Polynesian restaurant gives flower leis to both men and women; a continental restaurant gives an after-dinner cordial to each adult guest. (Local liquor laws should be consulted before giving alcoholic beverages gratis; some state liquor laws do not allow it.)

PUMP PRIMING

The owner of a medium-priced restaurant says: "See that big corner booth in the back? I try to get a group in there early in the evening, especially a gang that's out to celebrate. Then, I've got this gimmick. It's called a Yard of Ale. At the right time, I buy a round for the booth. The waiters make a big production out of carrying those crazy glasses through the dining room, and the bunch in the booth think it's really great. Then I start selling yards of ale all over the room, and it goes on all night. As soon as people see them, they want them. I make a terrific markup on them, and the giveaway costs me peanuts."

Pump priming, that is, giving away a small amount of food or drink in order to stimulate impulse sales, can be effective for certain types of items. Generally the items must be highly visible, even theatrical, in their presentation. The technique is most effective in occasion-type restaurants where people are out for a show as well as a meal.

10

Meeting the Public

So far we have discussed the technical and administrative aspects of dining room operation. Let's get the guest back into proper perspective. Too often the service staff can become so wrapped up in the technical aspects of service that the guest becomes "the chicken potpie on table 22" instead of a human being. When the employees are thinking of the customers as a hindrance to their work instead of the very reason that their jobs exist, something is very wrong.

SATISFYING NEEDS AND EXPECTATIONS

The restaurant business is a people business. It must satisfy the customer's needs today if it is to get his business tomorrow; and it needs his business tomorrow to stay in business.

How are his needs satisfied? Behavioral scientists say that

need satisfaction is the basis of all human behavior. Some needs may be obvious, but many are obscure. Abraham Maslow, the noted psychologist, proposed a hierarchy of needs. At the lowest level are physiological needs such as food, air, and shelter. Next are security needs—safety and freedom from fear. At the third and fourth levels are social needs—love and group belonging—and status needs—prestige and rank. At the top of Maslow's hierarchy is what he calls self-actualization; that is, the need to develop one's self and to use one's maximum potential.

There are other theories of human behavior, but Maslow's need hierarchy is useful in explaining what people really want when they go out to dine.

At the physiological need level, the guest is in search of food to satisfy his hunger. But he can satisfy that need at any restaurant in town as well as in his own home. Why should he satisfy it at a particular restaurant?

Perhaps it is because that restaurant satisfies his needs at the next level—security or freedom from fear. Every guest wants to know that the food he is served is safe to eat and that the rest rooms are clean. Also at this level is freedom from being robbed, a fear held by many who do not want to go into unsafe neighborhoods at night. A safe, well-lit parking lot may be needed if guests feel threatened.

At the next level on the hierarchy are social needs—group belonging and acceptance. What makes a guest become a regular? Probably a major factor is that he feels at home. He knows the staff and feels accepted and welcome. He belongs.

Next on Maslow's hierarchy are status needs—prestige and rank. Satisfying guests' needs at this level ought to be duck soup for the professional dining room staff. Could a woman leave the restaurant and exclaim "The service was really great; I feel like a queen"? Or could a man say, "Boy, they really treated me like a big shot"?

At the top of the need hierarchy is self-actualization. The restaurant patron striving to satisfy this need is often searching for the gourmet experience; for the ultimate wine or cheese; or for the latest "in" place to add to his roster of experiences.

For the service professional on the job, Maslow's theory

means first that, although guests are not usually operating on the basic need level, they may be temporarily very hungry or very tired (or even feeling ill), and perhaps beyond the point of being able to suppress that need in the interest of being civil.

Second, guests have a need for visible evidence of fire safety and security for themselves and their property. The restaurant should have adequate, visible safety and security provisions, such as clearly marked fire exits. Even more important is the need for clean premises. However, being technically clean is not enough. Since people make judgments based on what they see, the operation must also *look* clean. This includes clean, well-groomed employees; clean, well-supplied rest rooms; and neat work stations. In even the cleanest restaurants, the work areas can become messy during business. If these areas are visible to the guests, they should be kept neat and orderly throughout the serving period.

Third, guests want to feel that they are welcome—that they *belong* in the restaurant. The staff must communicate the feeling that guests are very important to them and that they are glad to see them. Even more important than belonging is recognition of the guest as a human being. The most threatening feeling a person can have is the feeling that he does not exist, which is what the staff is saying when they ignore someone. This can be even more devastating than a physical threat. It happens all too often when employees are busy conversing with each other and not paying attention to the area around them, or to the guests. The presence of guests should *always* be recognized in the work area, even if they are just passing through.

Fourth, the staff must go beyond simply recognizing the guests' existence; they must make them feel important. Everyone wants to feel worthy, significant, competent. Making guests feel important is basic to the job.

Fifth, on the self-actualizing level, there are always guests who want to try new foods or wines, to explore places in the area, to sound others out on subjects of interest. Service personnel should be knowledgeable about topics that relate to their jobs, and, if asked, be able to provide information or advice.

In addition to his collection of needs, the guest has a set of expectations that must be fulfilled. If they are not, he will have a bad response regardless of the quality of food or service. Expectations may be based on past experience at a restaurant, recommendations of friends, advertising, or just general ideas about dining out. If these expectations are not fulfilled, he will leave dissatisfied.

Furthermore, when the guest walks in the door, he comes from some place, some activity, and some experience. This experience may have been pleasant or unpleasant. He may have had an argument with the boss, a traffic ticket along the way, or lost out on a big sale. The guest may have spent the day with squabbling youngsters or on the job with an aggravating boss or client. Perhaps he just spent a half-hour looking for a parking space. You do not know what situation the guest has come from when he enters the door. He must be taken the way he comes, with all his needs, moods, and expectations.

There is a quality that professional service personnel should cultivate in themselves to enable them to deal with the unpredictable nature of the guest. It is the quality of *empathy* or the ability to put themselves in the other person's shoes and know what he is feeling. The person with empathy understands the embarrassment of an unsteady elderly person who has spilled something, the dismay of an inexperienced diner who ordered an unfamiliar dish he discovers he does not like, and the nervousness of a young man trying to impress an important date. Empathy can be thought of as a sensitive and accurate understanding of another person's feeling. The word "empathy" sounds like "sympathy," but the meanings are different. "Sympathy" implies a feeling of pity, and pity by itself is rather ineffectual. Understanding, on the other hand, or "empathy," tells the customer that his feelings are understood and that the staff would like to help. A helpful emphatic message by a member of the service personnel might be something like: "Oh what a shame. It is really disappointing (frustrating, maddening, etc.) when things like that happen. Let me get you something (make a phone call, take care of that, etc.)."

In business this is regarded as a customer-oriented approach. It is based on the recognition that the customer is the reason you are in business and that each customer's patronage is essential to the continuance of the business. This customer-orientation does not just happen.Management and supervisors must put the customer first and devote considerable time and effort to staff training. This important subject will be covered in chapter 13.

COMMUNICATING WITH GUESTS

If the needs of your guests are to be met, open communication is essential. People use two kinds of communication—formal, which involves the wording of the message, and informal, which involves how you send the message.

Informal communication includes how you look when you send the message, the tone of voice you use, and the body language or posture you have when sending the formal communication (see fig. 10-1). It is impossible not to communicate. Even when you are trying not to communicate, when you ignore a person, for example, you are sending a message: "I don't want to talk to you." Furthermore, behavioral scientists who have researched the matter say that informal messages are much more likely to be believed than formal messages, especially when there is a conflict between them.

The way you look and the setting you choose, (if you have a choice in the matter) send a message: a supervisor sits at a table near the dining room door, doing his paperwork. A guest approaches and waits in the doorway. The supervisor then puts down his pencil and goes to the door to greet the guest. The

10-1. A warm welcome from the hostess, who is using attending behavior— eye contact, positive body language, and a smile to communicate with guests.

formal message may be words of welcome, but the informal message is "You interrupted my paperwork, which is more important than greeting you." Paperwork must be done, but the supervisor should put guests first. It is not enough to respond to a guest's needs; you must *anticipate* his needs. The informal as well as the formal message must be "You, the guest, are the most important part of this business."

The need for good personal grooming was mentioned in chapter 5. A sloppy appearance sends an "I don't care" message, loud and clear. Body language also sends messages. Smiling; making eye contact (but not staring or a steady gaze); a posture with arms down or slightly open, a slight bend from the waist, chin-line level with the floor (not tilted up or down), and body squarely facing the person you are addressing—all communicate interest, openness, and welcome to others.

The tone of voice used can send an informal message that is exactly the opposite from the words used. A positive formal message sent with a negative vocal tone is "sarcasm." It is the negative message that is received, not the positive words.

The formal message—*what* you say—is, of course, very important. Techniques that professionals use to convey positive formal messages include the use of greetings, names, direct address, and common courtesy words.

Greetings recognize a person's presence and open up the communication channel. The greeting says "I respect you as a person, and I am friendly." It aims to make the person glad to be where he is.

Names should be used, often, whenever possible. Advertising people say that the words that get the most attention from customers are "sale," "free," and a person's name. The sweetest sound in the English language is the sound of your own name. If you are not sure how to pronounce a name, you should *ask*. Mispronouncing a name can be an insult. Asking indicates that you care enough to try to get it right. If the name is difficult, other people probably have trouble with it too, and the person will not be offended.

Direct address—using the word *you*—also conveys one's personal interest in a customer: "I'll check that for you"; "You have made a good choice"; "We have a very nice table for you."

Finally, the common courtesy words that you have heard since you were a child—"thank you," "please," and "you're welcome"—all indicate respect for the customers.

The following are taboos that should never be violated by the professional in his communication with guests:

- Negativities
- Problems
- Blame-placing
- Profanities
- Family affairs
- Talking about other guests

Negative thoughts and problems are downers. Even if it is just small talk, you should not be a killjoy. People go out to get away from problems. They do not want to hear about the staff's.

Avoid blame placing and making excuses. The guest does not want to hear about it. He is paying for service and he wants it as promised. This is a professional operation, and the guest expects it to perform that way. When blame is placed on someone in the organization, it reflects badly on the blamer. After all, he is part of the organization, too. The talk should be about what *can* be done, not who was to blame and what cannot be done.

It goes without saying, but the professional should never use profanity in his communication with guests. The guest may be using profanity, but the staff must not. It should also go without saying that "family affairs"—whatever is going on within the restaurant, whether it is politics or operating problems—should not concern the guest. For many people, there is a mystique about hotels and restaurants. They have some idea that this world is one long vacation or one big dinner party. If they find out that it is a business like any other business—with politics and problems—some of the fun goes out of their visit. Certainly, it is important to keep up the image.

Finally, guests should never be discussed with other guests. This is a violation of trust. When you talk about one guest to another, the second will wonder what you are going to say about him, and thereby loses confidence in you as a professional.

The underlying objection to all of these kinds of messages is that they shift the emphasis away from the guest to the employee, or at least, to the business. The goal must always be guest-oriented.

SERVING DISABLED GUESTS

With barriers to travel coming down, many disabled persons now have increased mobility; they are able to travel and to dine out, both for pleasure and on business. Furthermore, with the "graying" of the population, there are many more elderly people, forming a growing market for restaurant meals.

The federal government uses the term *handicapped*, but many professional people who work with disabled persons and many disabled persons themselves take strong exception to this term. In their view, society is handicapping people with disabilities by putting barriers in their way, preventing them from living fulfilled, independent lives. A handicap is a state of mind, not a physical condition.

The biggest barrier is not architectural—it is social acceptance. The goal is to learn to provide service to disabled people just as we provide service to able-bodied people—as whole individuals—and *then* to provide whatever special service is needed for their particular disability.

People with disabilities also have abilities, and that is what society tends to ignore. We sometimes assume that, because a person may have limited vision, he also has a limited mind, or that a person with limited mobility is dependent and must be treated as a child.

The staff should use the same degree of empathy with guests who have disabilities as they use with other guests. The problem is that it is very difficult for someone who has never experienced a disability to really know how to be empathic toward someone with one. This is especially true for a young, healthy employee, who has never had to depend on others for certain basic needs.

Such employees have nothing in their experience to relate this to. The closest many can come is in observing the daily life of someone in their own families—a relative who is getting old, for example.

The staff should relate to the disabled person as a human being, using all the skills of empathy they already know. This means recognizing the individual and greeting him directly, making eye contact—not asking others in the party information about him, talking as if he was not there.

Second, special assistance should be provided only to the extent that the disability requires it. When unsure about what assistance, if any, is required, you should ask if any special assistance is wanted. In many cases, the individual is quite capable of taking care of his own special needs, and does not want help. If it is wanted, you should ask how the person wants to be assisted, and do it his way, not yours. (He knows his own situation; the staff does not.) Often, intervention by others, even though well meaning, can be worse than no help at all.   ·

Blind Guests

When escorting a blind person, his hand should be placed on the escorter's elbow, and then he should be walked at a comfortable pace, obstacles avoided. He will walk a step behind the escorter. His arm should not be taken in an attempt to "steer" him. When the table is reached, the person's hand should be placed on the back of his chair. He will then seat himself. If the blind person is alone, he needs to be told what is on the menu and the prices. If he is with others, his companions will assist him.

If the person has a guide dog, the party should be put in a location where the dog can lay down out of the way. Guide dogs are exempt from health department regulations that bar animals in food-service establishments; in fact, in some states, it is against the law to refuse admission to a blind person with a guide dog.

Guide dogs should never be played with, petted, or fed while they are working (in harness).

When serving a blind person, one's presence should be announced when approaching the table and the person should be told what has been served and where it has been placed. The hands of the clock can be used: "Your filet of sole is at six o'clock, and the au gratin potato is at twelve o'clock. Your coffee is to the right of the plate at three o'clock."

Glasses and cups or soup bowls should not be filled to the brim.

One should announce it when removing dishes. Just asking the question "Are you finished with your salad?" for example, is a signal. Since blind guests cannot know when a service person is in the area, they have difficulty attracting the server's attention. Waiters should check frequently to see if anything is needed.

Blindness in and of itself does not affect manual dexterity. Unless the individual has other disabilities, he is probably quite capable of cutting his own food, unwrapping straws, and so on. Once the offer of any assistance has been made, he will take it from there. If he needs help, he will ask for it.

If a blind person is paying the bill, the waiter must tell him the amount. He should be asked if he would like to have it itemized. When he is brought his change, he will ask the amount of various bills, and he will then fold them in a particular way.

The staff should not be self-conscious about what words they use. Words such as "see" do not offend blind persons. The staff should smile when conversing with blind persons, as they would with sighted customers: the smile comes across in their voices.

Deaf Guests

When talking to a deaf person one should stand directly facing him, so that he can see lips and face clearly. Even though lip reading is not completely efficient, the guest may be able to read some of what is said. The waiter can confirm the order by pointing to items on the menu.

If someone else is signing for the deaf person, the person himself should still be addressed. To address the signer rather than the deaf person is akin to talking about the deaf person as if he was not there.

Persons who have been deaf since birth or an early age have had to learn to speak without the benefit of knowing how they sound, or how anyone else sounds. For this reason, their voices may sound strange—perhaps overly loud. For this reason, some deaf people do not like to speak in public, even though they are able to speak. This does not mean that they have below normal intelligence or that they cannot read.

Orthopedically Impaired Guests

Orthopedically impaired guests include those with impaired mobility or manual dexterity and people in wheelchairs. A person in a wheelchair can generally maneuver for himself, or will be maneuvered by the person escorting him. One should walk in front of the chair and clear any obstacles in its path; remove the regular chair from the table and put it out of the way. The wheelchair guest should be placed where he is accessible, but where the wheelchair is not blocking an aisle. Do not try to hide the party in the back of the room.

With a person on crutches, one should ask if he would like the crutches to be put away once he is seated. Some do and some do not.

A guest with a disability that affects hand movement may require different tableware from normal service. Examples might be a beverage served in a large tumbler, rather than a footed glass; a soup spoon instead of a fork; drinking straws for all beverages. The person should be asked if he would like his food cut up, and if so, how it should be cut.

Speech-impaired Guests

One should make an effort to understand a person with a speech impairment. One should repeat back what one thinks the person said, and then ask the person to repeat if there was a misunderstanding. He will be used to having to repeat himself, so one should not be embarrassed to ask several times.

Others in the group may translate, but one should continue to address the individual directly. (The translator should be thanked for his assistance, though.)

A paper and pencil should be available so the person can write down his request if all else fails.

HANDLING COMPLAINTS

In the past, many successful businessmen instilled a customer-oriented attitude in their employees with the slogan *the customer is always right*. A more modern version recognizes that employees have minds of their own: *the customer may not always be right, but he is never wrong*. The more enlightened approach eliminates the question of whether the customer is right or wrong because it does not matter. The object is to retain his goodwill and future business: *never let a dissatisfied customer leave the restaurant*.

Another customer-oriented approach is: *you never win an argument with a customer* because, if you win, you lose his future business, and there are very few restaurant operations that can afford to lose customers. Actually, the guest who complains is doing you a favor. First, he is giving you a chance to correct something that dissatisfied him. Second, he is alerting you to a situation that may have dissatisfied other guests as well. Many people will not complain; they just will not come back. And they may tell their friends about their unhappy experience. In that case, you will not see those people either. Word-of-mouth can be a very strong influence on sales, either positive or negative.

No matter how good service is and how well organized the business is, there will always be guest complaints. Each guest is an individual, and each has his or her own set of expectations. You can satisfy most people's expectations most of the time, but you cannot hope to satisfy all of them, all of the time.

Running a restaurant is a complicated business, and it takes a lot of people. As hard as you might try, you cannot control every single event taking place. Sometimes things go wrong; or at least, they do not go as well as you would like.

Then, too, guests do not live in a vacuum. Their moods and expectations are influenced by all kinds of experiences, past and present, beyond those they experience in the restaurant and with the restaurant staff. Sometimes those outside experiences can produce frustrations that are vented on the first handy target—the restaurant and its staff.

Finally, there are the "professional" complainers—people who fabricate a wrong, or make a big complaint out of a slight error in order to make a large claim against the restaurant. While such people do exist, , their numbers are small in comparison with the number of guests with legitimate complaints.

The complaining or angry guest can seem personally threatening. Being attacked or blamed for something in which you had no part is very unpleasant. Being blamed for something you could not help is not only unpleasant, it is frustrating.

The professional takes a different approach. The complaining guest is an opportunity to win a friend for the restaurant—one who is more apt to return in the future. Studies have shown that, when dissatisfied customers have had a satisfactory resolution of their complaints, they are more likely to be repeat customers than those who had no complaints. The professional also looks on the complaining customer as a challenge to his people-handling skills.

Aside from the "professional" complainer most guests complain because they are dissatisfied with some aspect of the service and they want it corrected. In other words, they want some action. Sometimes the situation that dissatisfied them cannot be corrected—it is over and done with. It may be possible to make an adjustment to the bill (which may be what the complainer is looking for), but the guest may really be complaining to vent emotion over the situation, and may not be looking for any action other than an apology.

Some guests complain in order to bring a situation to the attention of the management so that it can be corrected, and other guests will not experience it. These guests see themselves not as complainers, but as helpers, and want to be recognized as such. Sometimes people complain just to get some attention. People who are lonely sometimes use this approach to get someone to talk to them. Others may be used to interacting negatively with people, and can only talk about a situation in terms of what is wrong with it. Some people may use complaints to get some control over a situation in which they feel uncomfortable.

Every guest complaint should be seen as valid, regardless of whether you think it is justified or not. Obviously, the guest thinks it is valid, and he is the one who is paying the tab. Telling the guest that "nobody ever complained about that dish before" is telling him that he does not know what is good or that his taster is out of whack. Let's face it; everyone who eats food is an expert on good food, at least in his own eyes. Perhaps no one ever did complain about the particular dish. There is always a first time. Even in the best run kitchens there is always a possibility of human error. Do not assume that your kitchen is always perfect.

Offering excuses or attempting to blame someone else are other unprofessional responses to complaints. The complaining guest is not interested in explanations or blame placing. He is only interested in having the situation corrected. The woman who found a fly in her mornay sauce does not care to hear a long description of your pest control procedures. She only wants the offending dish replaced. The man who is unhappy about slow service is not interested in knowing that you are three people short today or that the boss is cutting back on the payroll. He has his own problems, and he does not want to hear about yours. He came to dinner to get away from problems for a little while, and he wants the service he is paying for.

Professionals in the business use a set of specific steps in handling complaints.

1. Allow the customer to vent emotion if it is present. Recognize it for what it is, and do not take it as a personal attack on you. (The "you" in "you idiots" is not aimed at you personally.)
2. Separate the facts from the feelings to identify the basis of the complaint. Listen for facts that will give insight into a solution. Anger may be suppressed; look for sarcasm or highly formal language. What the customer perceives as being true is *always* true . . . from his standpoint. This should

always be the frame of reference, not what is true from your standpoint.

3. Express empathy and a willingness to help. If the guest is expressing anger, acknowledge his right to be angry. If the company is truly at fault, admit it and apologize; but do not take the blame on yourself, unless you personally made the mistake. Do not put the blame on somebody else either. Keep the emphasis on solving the problem, not exploring the causes of it. Do not say something that you do not really feel—it will show as insincerity. Most of us can genuinely make statements such as "I'm sorry you were inconvenienced by this . . ." or "I'm sorry that this happened. . . ."

4. State the problem as you understand it and get agreement that you have understood it correctly. Use open-ended questions to fill in information that was not supplied. (If the person is really upset, give him a chance to cool down first.) Stay with the questioning until you have identified the real problem.

5. Offer one or more solutions. If none are acceptable to the guest, ask what would satisfy him. Allow the guest to keep his dignity intact (to "save face"). Know what the company policies are on guest complaints and what options you have.

6. Get agreement on a mutually acceptable solution. If you do not have authority to offer what the guest is seeking, call the manager.

7. Carry out whatever solution was agreed on and be sure it is done correctly. Stay with the problem, and do not let yourself get interrupted.

8. Follow up closely and make sure that everything goes as agreed on, and that the guest has no further cause for complaint. Make every effort to resolve the complaint while working with the customer.

In general, the professional approach is to establish a positive, courteous, open climate of problem solving—not a confrontation between guest and employee, but rather, guest and employee versus the problem. Be positive. Use positive language. For example:

Negative	*Positive*
Your complaint	Your concern or question
You have to . . .	Will you . . . please
I can't . . .	We can . . .
You should have . . .	Will you . . . please

The professional also inspires confidence in the guest that the problem will be resolved. This is done through positive language and attending behaviors:

Inspires no confidence	*Inspires confidence*
Okay, I've got that.	Let me read this back to be sure I've got it right.
That's a common problem.	I'll give this my immediate attention.
That's not my table.	We will take care of it right away.
We've had a lot of trouble with that.	I'll bring you a fresh one right away.
I don't know if I can help you with that.	Thank you for calling. Let me transfer you to Mr. Smith who can help you with that.
Don't worry about it.	I'll call you back within an hour and tell you how it will be handled.

Most guest complaints can be resolved with an apology and a corrective action by the supervisor or waiter. It may mean getting help for a waiter who is stuck, correcting a fault with a dish, or offering a replacement. If the complaint is by nature one that cannot be made right, you can show the guest that you really care about his patronage by picking up all or part of the check or by offering a free drink, dessert, or a bottle of wine. If the guest is ready to depart or is calling or writing to complain after the experience, you may ask him for another chance and offer a meal on the house (depending on the house policy, of course). Whatever the action, apologize and mean it.

Fortunately, frauds, professional cheats, and chronic complainers are few in number. Giving a free meal or drink to a professional cheat once in a while is much less costly than losing the future business of a guest with a legitimate complaint.

As mentioned earlier, a waiter may see a complaining guest as a threat—an insult to his ability to do his job, or perhaps even a threat to his personal integrity. Admittedly, there are people in this world who feel inadequate and insecure. They sometimes try to compensate by bullying people who are not in a position to fight back. These types are a real challenge, and that is the only way to deal with them . . . as a challenge to professionalism. Lowering oneself to that level by acting defensively is just what this kind of person wants. If one permits oneself to get angry with the person, one has lost control of the situation. The objective is to keep in control by providing every service necessary to satisfy him. Extra attention should be given to be sure he has absolutely nothing to complain about. Sometimes the insecure, complaining guest can be won over to become a steady guest and a loyal supporter once he learns to feel secure in the restaurant and knows he will receive all the attention he craves.

11

The Basics of Supervision

The professional dining room manager's biggest job is dealing with people—the guests he serves and the staff who provide this service. Although the various types of service require varying degrees of technical skills, the most important skill a dining room manager can have is the ability to deal with people. This chapter and the following one discuss the basic principles of supervision and motivation. These skills are important in dealing with employees.

WHAT IS SUPERVISION?

Supervision is often defined as "getting work done through people," but that is a bit oversimplified. Supervision is:

1. Seeing that work gets done.
2. Seeing that the work meets standards set by management.

3. Seeing that the work is done as efficiently as possible.
4. Seeing that the work is done in accordance with the policies and practices set by management.
5. Being held accountable or responsible for the results, day in and day out.

"Seeing that work gets done" is another oversimplification. It involves a number of activities:

1. Deciding what work is to be done.
2. Dividing the work into specific tasks.
3. Deciding how the tasks are to be performed—that is, the standards that must be met.
4. Obtaining any materials or equipment needed to perform the task.
5. Obtaining any information that may be needed to perform the task.
6. Assigning the tasks to specific workers.
7. Instructing them in what the task is and how it is to be performed.
8. Observing to be sure the task is performed according to instructions.
9. Determining the cause of any substandard performance and taking corrective action if necessary.

Although a bit abstract, this list of activities generally fits the job of the dining room supervisor.

First, what is the work that must be done? Customers must be served in the dining room seven days a week for breakfast, lunch, and dinner. The work may be classified as serving and clearing tables. The dining room manager determines the number of workers needed for each shift to serve the number of guests anticipated. Work may further be subdivided by dividing the tables into stations. Side duties such as stocking side stands and dining room housekeeping chores may be identified. Once these divisions of work are determined, they are assigned to the staff by means of the schedule. The dining room supervisor is also responsible for seeing that there is an adequate supply of linen, china, silverware, menus, and other equipment necessary to operate his room. He may be directly responsible for ordering the supplies and putting them into service, or his responsibility may end when he reports his needs to the manager. The supervisor must also keep informed about the activities of the other departments in the restaurant and about conditions outside that could affect his business. One specific type of information that he must provide to his staff daily is menu changes.

Staff instruction may consist of special instructions for a job that is to be performed once, such as a special service for a particular customer, a review of a new menu, demonstration of a particular procedure with the entire staff at a staff meeting, or a series of training sessions for a new employee.

During service the dining room supervisor is alert to the progress of service at each table in the dining room. He notes any lapse in service and receives customer complaints. Afterward he finds out why the lapse occurred and takes steps to prevent it from happening again. He may correct an individual employee, review a procedure with the entire staff, or work with the chef or kitchen manager to improve coordination between the dining room and the kitchen.

The preceding description gives a more accurate view of "getting the work done through people." There are several other aspects of supervision that must be emphasized. First, the supervisor must be willing to accept the responsibility for the operation of his department. As Harry Truman put it, "The buck stops here." When the performance of the department is not acceptable, the supervisor takes action to bring it up to standard. Second, the supervisor represents the management to the staff and to the public. He must be knowledgeable in the employment policies and practices of the house and be prepared to carry them out. Similarly, he must know the house policies regarding the handling of the public, such as when to "comp" a check, how to handle a complaint, and how to deal with an inebriated guest. Third, the supervisor also represents the staff to management. He must be aware of what his staff personnel are thinking and feeling about their job situation, and he must be able to communicate the staff morale to management. Fourth, the function of supervision is continuous. It is not a job that ends with the completion of a task or assignment. There is always the performance of work to be overseen, corrected, and planned for. The supervisor's job is never done.

AUTHORITY AND RESPONSIBILITY

In the preceding section the word *responsible* was used. By accepting responsibility, the supervisor assumes an obligation to perform certain functions; that is, he will see that the department operates in a certain way. If he does not carry out this obligation, the department will not function effectively and efficiently. Some of the dining room manager's specific responsibilities include the following:

1. Enforcing the policies and standards set by management. (Policies and standards will be defined below.)
2. Seeing that the desired quality of service is given.
3. Seeing that the operations in his department comply with all applicable laws (including labor laws, liquor laws if applicable, consumer protection laws, and so forth).
4. Maintaining safe conditions for both guests and employees.
5. Controlling costs within his department and protecting the property of the company.
6. Generating sales to the extent possible in his position.

The other side of the coin is authority. In order to fulfill his obligation, the supervisor must be able to make certain decisions and carry them out without asking the permission of his superior. Management delegates (gives to him) certain authority, the right to make certain types of decisions necessary in the operation of the department.

POLICY AND STANDARDS

In some cases, management may not wish to delegate complete authority. If they did, each department head would make independent decisions, and there would be no continuity between departments. When similar types of decisions are involved, management writes a policy. This is a guideline for handling such decisions so that the same decision is reached in each department when similar situations arise. For example, a personnel policy might state, "Each employee is entitled to two weeks vacation with pay after one year's employment."

Another area in which management will not wish to delegate complete authority is in the desired level of performance. Management will establish standards that each department must meet. Service quality standards were discussed in chapter 4. Other types of standards include cost standards (linen cost should not exceed $.XX per cover served), productivity standards (dining room staff productivity goal is XXX covers per manhour), or performance standards (orders shall be taken within XX minutes of seating the guest).

In large companies, standards are usually well defined and written down. Supervisors and managers are measured by how well their departments meet these standards.

In small businesses or individual restaurants, the standards may not be well defined or written down, but they still exist in the mind of the owner or manager. The dining room supervisor must try to interpret the level of performance desired or substitute his own standards.

LEADERSHIP

So far we have described what a supervisor does. How he does it may be called his leadership style. Behavioral scientists have identified four types of leaders: authoritarian, paternalistic, democratic, and participative.

Sometimes we find a fifth type—abdicative. The abdicative leader is really a nonleader. He lets his staff make the daily decisions about when and how they shall work. However, this does not mean the abdicative leader is idle. In fact, he may be the busiest person in the dining room—bustling about, bussing tables, serving coffee, and fetching silverware from the kitchen. This is a highly paid busboy rather than a true leader who gets the work done *through other people*.

The Authoritarian Leader

This type of leader is sometimes called an *autocrat*. He is the I-am-the-boss type. He makes all decisions arbitrarily without consulting anyone for information or opinions on the matter. He demands total obedience to his orders. He usually considers the employees greatly inferior to himself, assuming they are motivated only for their own personal gain and not interested in the requirements of the company or the job. He believes that people will do what he wants them to do only by fear of punishment. The authoritarian leader is often concerned with preserving his authority and administering discipline to those who do not obey his orders.

Paternalistic Leader

This is the father-knows-best type of leader. He differs from the authoritarian in that he cares about the welfare of the staff and wants them to be happy. The price he asks in return is that they accept all his decisions without question. He still does not value any contribution they may wish to make since he assumes they are not competent enough to make contributions. He may select certain individuals to be groomed for management, but he probably does not permit even them to contribute very much. He may provide a considerable amount of employee benefits, pay high wages, and offer good working conditions. However, they are all given by him unilaterally, with no participation in the planning or operation by the recipients of his gifts.

The Democratic Leader and the Participative Leader

The democratic leader identifies problems and refers them to his group to resolve by vote of the majority. This type of leader is usually much more successful than the autocrat or the paternalist in getting people to work for him. He involves the group in decisions that affect them. The problem with this type of leadership is that what the majority chooses to do may not be in the best interest of the business.

The participative style of leadership is getting much attention in the business press at present. The participative leader says to his subordinates, "Here is what has to be done. Tell me how you plan to do it. If it does not conflict with the policies and objectives of the company, you may go ahead and do what you propose. Furthermore, I will evaluate you on how well you achieve your own plan." This type of leadership may be more suited to supervision of managerial or professional level employees than to workers doing routine tasks, but the basic principles of participation and involvement of the individual are still applicable.

THE SUPERVISOR'S RESPONSIBILITIES TO THE STAFF

One supervisor says, "I believe I have certain responsibilities to my staff. If I don't fulfill those responsibilities, the department will look bad, and then I will look bad. It's strictly a matter of enlightened self-interest." These are the responsibilities this supervisor has to his staff:

1. To give people complete instructions and guidance on what is expected of them.
2. To provide a safe, clean working environment.
3. To have available the equipment and material people need to do their jobs.
4. To give a fair hearing to their suggestions and complaints.
5. To correct any work performance that is not meeting standards. (It is unfair to those who are doing good work to tolerate substandard performance in others.)
6. To recognize good performance and let the employee know where he stands.
7. To have personal respect for the dignity of each individual.
8. To be fair in making judgments and enforcing rules and regulations.
9. To understand that workers have a life outside of work, that their values and priorities may not be the same as the

boss's, and that they are not available on demand to do the boss's bidding.

10. To see that all members of the staff are paid a fair and living wage.

DISCIPLINE VERSUS CORRECTIVE ACTION

Discipline is often thought of as punishment for past behavior. The parent punishes the child to impress on him that certain behavior is bad and must not be repeated in the future. Unfortunately, on-the-job discipline can sometimes be revenge for past behavior rather than prevention of certain future behavior.

What one should really be concerned with is corrective action, the last step in the sequence of activities that constitute supervision. The object is to motivate the individual to a desirable performance in the future, regardless of past performance. Vindictive disciplinary action by the supervisor is more likely to cause resentment and a negative response.

To correct undesirable behavior, the supervisor must first discuss the situation privately with the individual and listen to his side of the story. There may be circumstances that make a disciplinary action inappropriate. An infraction of a rule may have been unintentional or the result of a misunderstanding. Poor work performance may indicate a need for additional training rather than a reprimand.

When criticism or a reprimand is in order, it should be given in a positive manner. Correct the specific behavior, not the person. Give him a chance to save face and maintain his dignity. Destroying a person's self-respect and confidence will not improve his work performance. Obviously this means having your talk in private, in an environment free of interruption. It also means treating the matter as completely confidential. Do not just chew out the individual on the fly. Be specific about the behavior that prompted your action. Be sure you handle his situation exactly the same as you would handle it with another person. Whether the staff is unionized or not, make a written record of your warning with the particulars and send a copy to the office to be put in the personnel files. You should also note it in your logbook.

Usually one interview is enough to resolve the situation. However, if the behavior is repeated, further action is required. The group-oriented leader will try to give every benefit of the doubt to the employee. He asks himself whether he made the situation absolutely clear to the employee. Could he have misunderstood the last conversation? Is there a language problem? It may be that the individual is just in the wrong job. Some people are just not comfortable in dealing with the public but can work well in back of the house. Others may not be able to deal with the stress of a rush period and need a more even-paced work environment.

Labor turnover is very costly in any organization. Throwing people out like tissues destroys the morale of those who remain. If an employee thinks he might get the ax tomorrow, he is not motivated to top performance today. A competent, skilled employee will decide to take his chances elsewhere rather than risk being fired. The supervisor who has a high turnover among his staff is probably doing something wrong.

12
Motivation and Job Performance

The *how* of getting work done is really getting people to do the work. This is best accomplished by getting them to want to do the work. In other words, they must be motivated.

Motivation is not manipulation. Motivation is providing a means of satisfying the individual's needs in a way that fills the needs of the business as well. The manipulator is only concerned with getting people to behave in a way that satisfies his own needs without regard for the other person's needs or interests.

The individual we want to motivate—the employee—is not an automaton. He is a total person, an individual with many parts to his being:

- Physical health
- Mental health
- Emotional health

- Educational background
- Home life and family
- Financial status
- Religious, moral, and social values
- Personality
- Career or job expectations
- Hobbies and interests
- Future expectations
- Abilities and skills

The supervisor must deal with the total person and with the wants and needs created by all the aspects of his being.

In chapter 10 Maslow's hierarchy of needs was discussed. It represents one way of understanding human behavior. How does this theory apply to people on the job? First of all, most people work for one primary reason—to make a living; that is, to satisfy their physiological needs by providing food, shelter, and clothing for themselves and their families. Where they work, what they work at, and how they work are factors in higher-level need satisfaction. Once an individual is earning a wage adequate to provide him with the necessities, his basic needs are satisfied (although for reasons of status or self-actualization he may wish to satisfy his housing, food, and clothing needs on a higher, more expensive level).

Once a person's physiological needs are met, he moves on to the next level—security and freedom from fear. This is a need that motivates people to join unions for job security and to obtain benefits such as sick pay and health insurance.

The next level on the need hierarchy is love, belonging, and group acceptance. Peer group acceptance is a very powerful need, and it cannot be satisfied by management. Every work group forms its own peer structure with its own leader. Knowing who the peer leader is and winning his support can be effective in winning support from the total group.

Management can appeal to belonging needs by including employees in the decision-making process and keeping them informed of developments in the company. Participation and sharing of information are effective in building a spirit of cooperation and team work, which is what belonging is all about.

The need for prestige and status is fairly well recognized in business. Among hourly employees, recognition through gifts (such as pins or tie clasps for length of service), write-ups in the company paper of achievements on and off the job, and promotion of qualified employees to higher level positions are common practices.

Recognition of good performance is always rated highly when workers are asked what they want from their jobs. It is also one of the easiest (and least expensive) needs for the company to meet. Unfortunately, managers often forget that the most effective form of recognition is a few words of approval and appreciation for a job well done.

At the top of the need hierarchy is self-realization, the need to develop one's potential to its fullest and to use one's skills and abilities. One attribute is pride of workmanship. Everyone wants the satisfaction of knowing he does his job well. The worker who does not care about his performance is probably in the wrong job.

Maslow's hierarchy explains why simply paying higher wages is not an effective way to motivate personnel. When you reward an employee with a merit increase, it is for past performance. The individual is now able to satisfy his physiological needs on a higher level, but he does not relate past wage increases to his future performance on the job.

Frederick Herzberg, another psychologist, concluded from some research studies that there are two sets of factors that affect job satisfaction and performance: job content factors and what he called hygiene or maintenance factors. Job content factors had to do with growth, achievement, recognition, and advancement. These all had positive effects on job satisfaction when they were present but did not produce much dissatisfaction when they were absent. Hygiene or maintenance factors, which include wages, working conditions, supervision, status, security, company policy, administration, and other basic biological needs worked the opposite way. When these needs were not satisfactorily met, strong dissatisfaction resulted. When they were met, however, they did not contribute in any great degree to job satisfaction. From his findings, Herzberg developed the concept of job enrichment, that is, structuring each job to include opportunities for individual responsibility, achievement, recognition, growth, and advancement—the factors he identified as contributing to job satisfaction and therefore offering the greatest potential for motivation.

MOTIVATION AND LEADERSHIP

Let's relate Maslow's need hierarchy to motivational methods used by various styles of leadership described in the preceding chapter.

Authoritarian Leaders

The authoritarian's primary method of motivation is fear of punishment. He demands obedience without question. The approach may be suited to short periods of stress and crisis when there is not time to go into all the details of the issue. In a restaurant during the heavy rush period, the supervisor says to the busboy, "Water glasses!" That is a direct order to go and get glasses from the dishroom, an order issued in a stress situation. In times of stress, most people accept this type of leadership and may even expect it, but it is far less acceptable under ordinary conditions. Then the primary response is to do only what is necessary to avoid punishment. There is no satisfaction of higher-level needs. Since few people these days are forced to exist on the freedom from fear level, they find this situation unsatisfactory in a job situation, and they will look elsewhere for employment if they can.

Paternalistic Leaders

The paternalist uses rewards, often in the form of parental approval, as his method of motivation. He has moved up one level on the hierarchy and appeals to the need for acceptance and love. For some people, especially those who are insecure, this can be an effective appeal. The paternalist who can inspire confidence in his managerial and technical ability often becomes a teacher or mentor for young people just entering and learning the business. If the paternalist is not particularly able and successful, his subordinates will become impatient with his mediocre leadership and their inability to make their own contribution. The paternalist denies the capabilities of those under him and cuts them off from participation and from self-development and advancement. When individuals are treated like children, they respond like children, operating on the fear-of-punishment level.

Democratic and Participative Leaders

Democratic and participative leaders generally have more success in motivating people because they appeal to higher level needs. They involve their staff in making decisions that will affect them. When the employee is involved in the management process, he becomes an important member of the team. The participative leader especially appeals to the self-actualization need on an individual basis.

Successful supervisors use a combination of leadership styles, depending on the situation and on the individuals involved.

FRUSTRATION AND TYPICAL RESPONSES

What happens when needs are not satisfied? The answer is in one word—frustration. If this frustration is not released, the result is aggression. We have all heard the classic chain reaction:

1. The spouse argues with the boss at breakfast.
2. The boss yells at the workers.
3. The worker goes home and fights with the spouse.
4. The spouse hollers at the kid.
5. The kid goes out and kicks the dog.

How do people release frustration before it becomes aggression? One response is to escape, that is, leave the scene. This may take the form of quitting one's job or walking out.

Every dining room supervisor sooner or later has the experience of having a waiter or waitress walk out on his station in a stressful situation. The waiter is leaving the scene to avoid releasing his aggression in the wrong way. The other alternative may be to punch someone in the nose. Other types of escape are daydreaming and apathy. The apathetic worker has ceased to care. He finds ways outside of his job to satisfy his belonging and self-actualization needs.

Another response to frustration is alternative behavior, that is, taking a detour to find some other way to satisfy a frustrated need. For example, if there is not enough silverware to go around, the staff will start to hoard it and take it from each other's stations in order to keep their tables set up. Another detour-type response is the grapevine. When management withholds information from the employees about matters that concern them, a grapevine develops. This informal information system feeds on rumors, tidbits, and misinformation.

The most satisfactory response to frustration is problem-solving behavior—that is, taking direct steps to resolve the conflict, remove the frustration, and satisfy a need. In the example above, problem-solving behavior would be a representative of the staff going to the boss to present their need for more silverware.

When these alternative responses to frustration are blocked, the aggression response is all that is left. Aggression may be physical violence against individuals or property, or it may be verbal violence and hostile behavior. If this type of behavior becomes evident to the guests in the dining room, it must be defused. Most individuals will attempt to inhibit such behavior publicly, but inhibited aggression becomes an even stronger force.

A person may release his aggression against himself instead of releasing it against others. He may drive his car recklessly and have an accident, develop headaches or ulcers, or try to drown his troubles in alcohol.

The supervisor is obviously not in a position to eliminate all causes of frustration in an employee's environment, but he must be prepared to deal with it when it affects staff performance.

When you are dealing with hostility and aggression, the immediate task is to defuse the situation, calm down the individual, and get his mind back on his work. Where more than one person is involved, get them apart and cool them off separately. It is vital that the supervisor keeps his cool. An angry boss only adds more fuel to the fire. Do not blame, condemn, or attempt to deal with the causes of the aggression as long as the participants are still hot.

Later on, take the time to sit down and listen calmly to the employee's side of the story and gather all the facts. The simple act of listening receptively without interruptions often relieves many pent-up frustrations and permits the person to examine his situation more rationally.

The first explanations given are usually not the real causes. At this point the supervisor must decide how deeply he wants to delve into factors that may be outside of the job situation. Very few supervisors are qualified to be guidance counselors and should not attempt to play that role. They can do more harm than good. If an employee needs help in dealing with personal problems, it is best to refer him to a professional counselor.

The supervisor's role should be to listen with understanding, without blaming or judging, without trying to impose or suggest a solution to the individual's problem. Allow the employee to sort out his thoughts and reach his own solution.

As for the job situation, work-related complaints should not be dismissed simply because "it was something else that was really eating him." These complaints are most likely real sources of frustration and should be investigated. If you are unreceptive to such complaints, you will turn off the flow of communication and future confidences. If an employee does not feel free to discuss a small complaint with his supervisor, he may bottle it up until it erupts as a big problem in the future. If the troops aren't doing a little griping now and then, something is wrong. It is the supervisor's job to find out what's bothering them and to resolve little problems before they become big ones.

A CUSTOMER-ORIENTED ATTITUDE

In an earlier chapter the customer-oriented attitude was discussed. How do managers motivate their employees to care about their customers? All the handbooks and training classes in the world are not going to change an individual's attitude toward people.

Behavioral scientists say that attitudes are very complex bundles of assumptions that influence the probability of behaving in a certain way. Those assumptions include values, feelings, and beliefs about ideas, people, things, and situations. An attitude has several parts:

- *Beliefs:* The part that is "fact" (known to be "true"). One person's facts and truths may not be another person's facts and truths.
- *Feelings:* How one feels about the fact or truth and the strength of that feeling.
- *Behavior:* The likelihood of a particular behavior occurring as a result of beliefs and feelings about those beliefs. This depends in part on how important the feelings and beliefs are to the individual in this particular setting.

Attitudes can be changed in several ways. Changing the beliefs or the feelings about the belief can change the likelihood of behavior. Changing the behavior can, as a result, change both the beliefs and the feelings. This is the basis of behavior modification theory.

Here is one example of how an attitude works:

- *Belief:* They are making money in this place hand over fist. Look at the prices they charge.
- *Feelings:* They talk about cutting out waste, but they really do not mean it. Anyway, they make enough profit. Look at the big cars the owners drive. Besides, it is really nicer for the guests when we give them extra portions of butter, rolls, and jam, and we get better tips.
- *Behavior:* Efforts of management to control food cost will not be effective, and the staff will continue to waste food.

Here is an example pertaining to customer service:

- *Belief:* The most important thing in this job is getting the food out fast.

- *Feeling:* Customers who interrupt me and keep me from being fast and efficient are a real pain in the neck.
- *Behavior:* Guests with special requests or who need extra time and service are either ignored or treated in a cold, possibly rude manner.

Here are techniques that a manager can use to change attitudes like this:

1. Deal with the beliefs. Unlike the belief expressed above, "the most important thing in this job" should be to satisfy the customers. Communicating this truth is partly a function of training, but more a function of constant demonstration. Managers must place customer satisfaction as their top priority every day. Furthermore, provide feedback. Read the guest comment cards and letters—both good and bad—to the staff. Let them know what guests say and what is important to *them*.
2. Deal with the feelings. Some guests *are* a pain in the neck—and worse. That cannot be changed, but employees can change the way they feel about such guests. This is discussed further in chapter 13.
3. Deal with the behavior. In chapter 10, specific behavioral standards were discussed. Keep discussions about performance on specifics—not about general attitude.

Developing a concerned, customer-oriented staff starts with the manager. If managers are not customer-oriented, the employees will not be either. But it goes beyond this. Managers must also care about the employees and treat them as mature, responsible members of the team. The way in which managers treat their employees quickly becomes the way in which the employees treat each other and the guests. It is the manager who creates the atmosphere in every restaurant. Whether he is open and supportive, small-minded and petty, or cold and self-centered, his way of interacting with people will filter through to the supervisors and the staff.

In a previous chapter human needs were discussed. Management must fulfill the employee's needs before the employee is able to meet the guest's needs. A waiter cannot be warm and gracious to the guest in the dining room when he has just been verbally attacked by the manager in the kitchen.

Finally, managers must require the customer-oriented attitude and performance 100 percent of the time. If you do not ask for it, you will not get it. Set the standard high, but be willing to bend a little once in a while. You may not get 100 percent performance all the time, but you will come much closer to it than you would have if you did not ask at all.

Job Performance Problems

Job performance is a combination of knowledge, skill, and attitude—or specifically, an attitude of willingness. Knowledge and skill, and, to a lesser degree, attitude, are affected by training. Some job performance problems, however, are not affected by holding more training classes.

Sometimes the problem is operational. There are barriers that prevent employees from performing as they are supposed to. One of the objectives of employee involvement programs is to identify such barriers and remove them. In addition, when employees are involved in finding solutions, they are much more likely to accept the resulting changes that affect the way they work.

Sometimes employees are in effect rewarded if they do not do something, rather than if they do something. It takes extra effort to sell desserts and after-dinner drinks. Incentive selling programs that reward the best salesmen can overcome this inertia. Thus, one technique for improving job performance is to change the reward structure.

Another technique that can affect job performance is called a *job aid*. For example, posting price lists in strategic places aids employees in pricing guest checks properly. A small card that can be carried in the pocket can be used as a memory jogger on wines or menu items, or even on house policies and procedures.

13
Training

Why train? Training is expensive. It ties up supervisors; takes workers away from their jobs; and requires space, training materials, and sometimes expensive equipment. After all this costly training, chances are the employee will quit anyway.

The answer is, of course, that while you have the employee, you have a trained employee, and trained employees are more productive than untrained ones. In the preceding chapters some of the factors related to job satisfaction and labor turnover were discussed. Individuals who are trained in their jobs are certainly more likely to derive satisfaction from doing their jobs well. They are also less likely to experience the frustration of job demands and situations they have not been prepared to cope with. For this reason, training itself works to reduce problems arising from high labor turnover.

Training should also be viewed as a long-term investment from which the company should get a return. There must be a measurable benefit from a training program, though this return may not be expressed in dollar savings. For example, one objective of a training program is to improve the quality of work performed and raise it to the established standards. This should reduce customer complaints and increase the volume of business. As employees become more proficient in their jobs, productivity and morale improve and staff turnover is reduced. The overall effect is reduced labor costs. With proper training, employees in lower-echelon jobs can be upgraded to more skilled positions as the need arises. A policy of advancement from within also contributes to a high level of staff morale. In addition, training reduces waste, breakage, and accidents.

In the past, training of service employees usually took one of two forms—the sink-or-swim method,or the buddy system. The sink-or-swim method is nontraining. It assumes a new employee is an experienced worker and can walk right into the job and start work. The employee may be experienced but not in *this* restaurant and not serving *this* menu.

The sink-or-swim method, which is still used in some restaurants, obviously does not provide the new employee with the information he needs to do his job properly. What is worse, it says something about the attitude of management toward employees. It tells the new employee that he is not important; management cannot be bothered with him. As we have seen in the previous chapter, this is not the way to motivate an individual on the job. Total negligence of the training responsibility is a major cause of high labor turnover.

In the buddy system the new employee is assigned to follow an experienced employee for a few days before he is given a station of his own. During that time, the experienced worker is supposed to train him. This system relieves management of the job of training and places it on an employee. Some employees may consider it a compliment to be a trainer, but others may consider it a burden, especially if it cuts down on their tips. The real problem with this method is that few workers are good trainers. It is even harder when they are trying to perform their own jobs at the same time. Few people can do two jobs at once and do both well. Something has to suffer—usually, the trainee.

There is another disadvantage to this system of training.

Waiters and waitresses as a group are quite mobile, moving frequently from job to job and from town to town. Through their different work experiences, they develop a set of work habits and ways of serving that may or may not be acceptable to their current employer. Any bad habits they bring to their present job are usually passed on to new employees they train. Because of this, some operators prefer to hire completely inexperienced people and train them in their own style of service, thus creating a need for some type of formalized training program. Since there are always new employees entering the organization, this training must be ongoing.

A PROFESSIONAL APPROACH TO TRAINING

A more professional approach to training involves several different types of programs, each having different objectives and using different techniques. Job behavior is the result of a combination of knowledge, attitude, and skills. All three are necessary for proper job performance, and the training program must deal with all three. However, as discussed in chapter 12, attitude is only partially affected by training.

The first type of training is a new employee orientation. This kind of training provides the employee with basic information about the company, its policies, and its procedures. Its objective is primarily attitudinal—to create a positive attitude about the company and the job.

The second type of training provides technical skills—how to set a table or serve specific menu items. It provides a combination of knowledge and skill.

The third type of training is behavioral. It deals with the manner in which the service is performed, focusing mainly on salesmanship, communications skills, and the handling of emotions.

New Employee Orientation

The purpose of new employee orientation is to give the new employee information about the organization and his place in it. The technique is primarily information-giving (see fig. 13-1).

NEW EMPLOYEE ORIENTATION CHECKLIST

done:

_____ 1. Instruct the new employee to report at least one hour earlier than usual on the first day, so you will have time for the orientation.

_____ 2. Make the new employee feel welcome; give him or her your undivided attention for the time of the orientation.

_____ 3. Check payroll and personnel forms; get any filled out or corrected that are not complete. (Application, W-2, benefit cards, time card, etc. Be sure you have completed the payroll-change form to enter the new employee into the computer.) Explain how and when people get paid.

_____ 4. Assign locker.

_____ 5. Issue uniform; explain uniform policies and procedures for getting clean uniforms.

_____ 6. Conduct a tour of the restaurant, including kitchen, locker room, linen room, all dining rooms, bar, and banquet rooms.

_____ 7. Introduce employee to supervisors, kitchen staff, coworkers. Describe the organization; not all managers are available for introductions at the same time.

_____ 8. Issue a copy of employee handbook and job description. Review the following points in the handbook:

The schedule, procedures for checking in and checking out, phoning in if late or ill

Policies on employee meals and breaks

Policies on liquor service

Rules on tip-reporting

Policies on customer service

Benefits program

_____ 9. Explain sidework assignments.

_____ 10. View welcoming video.

_____ 11. Express confidence that the new employee will be a good addition to the organization.

13-1. A checklist for a new employee orientation.

The overall objective of new employee orientation is to communicate the values and standards of the organization, especially the message that people, including the new employee, are important and valued. Another objective of this type of training is to communicate to new people what is expected of

↳ new employee oreintation - give them basic knowledge about their restaurant

them and what standards of behavior and performance they will be held to.]

When large numbers of employees are hired, new employee orientations are done in groups that meet in classroom-type situations, usually with a training specialist from the personnel department. The employees learn about the company—its benefits, policies, work rules, and general personnel procedures. In large organizations, new employees may be shown a video about the organization, with a brief welcome from the president of the company. Later, the new employees are introduced to the people they will be working with and given a tour of the place they will be working in. They receive copies of the organization's employee handbook, which reinforces the information already given about the company's policies and rules. (Employee handbooks are discussed in chapter 14.)

[Usually, however, there are only one or two new employees at a time in a local restaurant operation. The orientation is then done on an individual basis. The personal contact must be supplied by the supervisor instead of a training specialist, although in larger operations this may be supplemented with a short video welcoming the new person to the organization. It is important that time be spent with new employees and that this contact is friendly, making the individual feel welcome. In addition, an employee handbook should be provided, regardless of how small the operation is. The new employee's initial impression of the organization and the people in it will have a strong impact on his or her attitude about the job and subsequent performance standards.]

→ Employee orientation is the first impression that a person has of your business as an employee

Technical Skills Training

The second type of training is technical skills training. This phase of the training program gives the employee the "how-to" knowledge—the specifics of how each task is to be performed. For service employees, this type of training emphasizes the steps of service, the table settings, and the details of service, as described in chapter 4.

Although technical skills training is aimed primarily at new employees, some managers rely on an ongoing schedule of short brush-up sessions to maintain high performance standards. In addition, special sessions on the service of new menu items are usually scheduled when there is a major menu change.

Technical skills training consists of providing information about the task, demonstrating the task, watching the trainee perform the task, and providing feedback on both the good aspects of the performance and on those points that need improvement.

One formal method of training in technical skills is JIT—Job Instruction Training. JIT was originally developed to train unskilled defense workers quickly during the Second World War. The JIT motto was, "If the worker hasn't learned, the instructor hasn't taught!" It is still used as the basis for training programs in most industries. JIT breaks down instruction into four steps:

1. Prepare the worker. Put him at ease and find out what he already knows about the job. Get him interested in learning the job.
2. Present the operation. Tell, show, illustrate, and question carefully and patiently. Stress key points. Instruct clearly and completely, taking up one point at a time.
3. Try out performance. Test him by having him perform the job. Have him tell and show you; have him explain key points. Ask questions and correct errors. Continue until *you* know he knows.
4. Follow up. Put him on his own. Designate someone he can go to for help. Check frequently. Encourage questions. Get him to look for key points as he progresses. Allow the coaching and close follow-up to taper off.

Before teaching, the instructor must prepare. JIT lists four preparation steps for the instructor:

1. Set a timetable. How much do you expect him to learn and how soon?
2. Break down the job. List principal steps. Pick out key points.
3. Have everything ready—the proper equipment, materials, and supplies.
4. Arrange the work place just as you expect the worker to keep it.

[handwritten margin note, left: JIT and its use]

[handwritten margin note, left bottom: what must be done to prep area before training]

teach employees
personal skills ⌐

Behavioral Skills Training

The third type of training deals with behavioral skills, such as salesmanship, customer relations, communications skills, and stress-handling. Although some knowledge is provided to form the basis of the behavior, most of the training consists of practicing and evaluating new types of behaviors. Attitude is affected when the employee is able to obtain positive, reinforcing responses from guests.

This type of training is relatively new in the restaurant industry, but is rapidly catching on. Service jobs involve what is being called "emotional labor," as opposed to physical labor or intellectual labor. Part of the job includes changing or reinforcing guests' emotional feelings. The catch is that to do this, the employee's own feelings are involved.

smile schools ⌐

Some customer service training programs have been nicknamed "smile schools" by employees who have experienced them. Smile schools deliver sermons on the importance of the customer and implore employees to "smile, smile, smile." Some interpersonal skills may be taught, but the employee's own emotions are ignored. Employees are told to have a customer-oriented attitude, but the bases for the attitude are ignored.

✓

The Professional Hospitality Skills Program of the Quality-service Group (a training and consulting firm for professionals in the hospitality industry) teaches the skills of empathy—verbal and nonverbal communications skills (described in chapter 10)—but goes even further in providing the employee with a way of dealing with his own feelings, especially anger and poor self-image. Stress-handling techniques are also taught. This program does not attempt to change attitudes, but rather to teach behaviors as job skills. Attitudes toward customer service do change as employees experience positive feedback from guests, reduced stress levels, and improved self-image.

employee/guest
interaction ⌐

Responsible Beverage Service Training

Another type of behavioral training is a responsible beverage service program. Because of public concern, many restaurant operators who serve alcoholic beverages are conducting training programs on responsible beverage service. Some insurance companies provide an added incentive for conducting such training through lower premiums for liability insurance.

Such training programs generally address three issues:

1. Obtaining a change in server behavior.
2. Knowing when to intervene.
3. Learning how to intervene effectively.

Server training programs give information on drinking habits, attitudes toward alcohol past and present, the physiological effects of drinking, the scope of the drunk-driving problem, and the legal liability aspects. This is the "awareness" step, and it is designed to provide information that will change attitudes and foster the tendency to behave responsibly in serving alcoholic beverages. Only a small part of the information provided in this step is directly related to job performance.

The second part of responsible beverage service training is teaching when to intervene in service to a guest. This requires judgment, and the training should provide some standard of comparison upon which to make that judgment.

The third part of the training focuses on intervention skills. These include decision making—selecting a course of action to take and knowing how to implement it. Implementation primarily requires verbal skills—what to say and how to say it.

REQUIREMENTS OF A SUCCESSFUL TRAINING PROGRAM

To be successful, a training program must have a specific objective. Without it, the trainers will be operating in a vacuum. We have already mentioned some typical training program objectives:

- To improve the quality of service and raise it to the established standards
- To reduce customer complaints
- To increase productivity and reduce labor cost
- To reduce waste
- To reduce accidents

These objectives are closely related to the basic goals of the company. In fact, training specialists state that without the support of top management, no training program can be successful. Training must be supported at all levels of the organization, from the top management who authorize the investment to the line supervisors who carry out the program. Without ongoing training, the survival and growth of the enterprise is in jeopardy.

Another requirement of a successful training program is a motivated trainee. No training can be successful if the employee does not want to learn. He will be motivated, however, if he believes he will benefit in a direct way. Of course, new employees want to learn so that they will be able to perform the job properly.

A program introduced at an established operation may meet resistance from long-timers. These employees may perceive the program as something new and strange, representing a radical change from the way they have been doing things. They may also feel insulted that their years of experience are being ignored and that they are being classed as rank beginners. Either way, a new training program is seen as a threat. Management must present a training program as having a direct benefit for both experienced and new employees. Better service means more business and larger tips.

A successful training program also needs supervisors who know how to train. It may mean that the first step in implementing the program is to train the trainers.

Finally, the program needs a detailed plan and a time schedule. It should not be allowed to ramble along with training sessions scheduled when time is available. In addition, there should be follow-up to insure that the objectives of the program are met.

TRAINING METHODS

The teaching methodology will have an impact on the effectiveness of the training. A number of methods are available for transmitting knowledge and developing job skills. They are:

1. Written materials or an audio cassette. Used individually, these provide one-way transmittal of information, which presents no opportunity for the learner to ask questions or practice skills. Limited feedback may be available, however, if the material contains a self-test on the information being provided.
2. Lectures. The lecture method assumes a group of individuals are being trained at one time. Lecturing is a verbal transmittal of information that generally allows for some interaction with the lecturer.
3. Group discussion. This permits the learners to interact and become involved with the material. The technique is more often used with behavioral training, although discussions of job skills can also be beneficial.
4. Videos. Videos provide animated, visual information. The information flow is all one way, however. Video is recommended for illustrating behaviors, such as body language or effective beverage-service techniques, or for providing standards that servers can use in judging degrees of guest inebriation, for example. Video can also be used to communicate attitudinal messages from corporate executives and spokesmen.
5. Case study. Used mainly in behavioral training situations, such as responsible beverage service or the handling of difficult guests. Case study permits learners to practice choosing the course of action to be taken in particular situations.
6. Games, role plays, and simulations. These permit the learner to try out all the new skills in a controlled environment and to get feedback. These techniques are useful for teaching both technical and behavioral skills. The practice of having trainees serve meals to supervisors is a form of simulation.
7. "Real time performance" under supervision. This technique is probably the most commonly used one for teaching technical skills. For it to be successful, however, positive as well as negative feedback is essential.

Skills are not mastered in a few hours of class time. Typically, there is a learning curve, rapid at first, then a leveling off for a time, followed by a slower rate of improvement. A bad experience may provide a demotivator that must be overcome. Supervisors should be checking their floor personnel periodically and reviewing their progress.

Tasting Sessions

There is one additional training method that is unique to restaurant service operations. That is the tasting session. Some operators do not use tasting sessions, because they think they are too costly. However, it is hard to understand how dining room personnel can possibly be enthusiastic salesmen for wines or menu items if they do not themselves know how these items taste.

Tasting sessions should be conducted on a professional basis, and not as a free-for-all. The items to be tasted are first discussed, and major points about their flavors described. If wines are being tasted, the discussion should include recommendations as to what menu items each wine goes well with. If food items are being tasted, the discussion should include information about the ingredients and method of preparation. Generally, only a limited number of items are tasted in a single session, since the palate can suffer from "sensory overload." Four to six wines and six to eight food items are about the most that should be scheduled for a tasting session.

Employees should be requested not to smoke or eat prior to the tasting session. The items to be tasted should be presented in a sequence—white wines before reds; cold foods before hot; with a range of mild flavors to strong. Water and perhaps bland, unsalted crackers should be available for cleansing the palate after tasting each item.

TRAINING MATERIALS

There are a number of very good training materials and films available. The *Bibliography and Training Materials* appendix includes a list of sources for food-service training materials and training consultants. These materials provide general instruction in restaurant service, although they may not be suited to a particular operation. They may be used in conjunction with a trainer-conducted program or in individual training conducted by supervisors in the local operation.

Most of the "off-the-shelf" training materials deal with job or technical skills. These can be used for training employees who have never been servers before. However, most restaurants, including all theme and specialty operations, must develop some customized supplementary materials for their particular menu and method of operating. For details of service, some operators take color photographs of each item on the menu, with its proper accompaniments, and post them in the kitchen area as a job aid. Videos have proven to be effective for this use, even for smaller operations. They are efficient to use and relatively easy and inexpensive to make—an important consideration when materials must be updated periodically.

Some of the commercially available films may be suitable to supplement a new employee orientation program, but the employee handbook is more often the primary training vehicle. For orientations conducted by supervisors, some companies use a new employee orientation checklist to ensure that all points are covered. When the list has been completed, the employee and the supervisor may be required to sign off on the form, and it is put into the employee's personnel file. This can provide proof in the future that certain policies and work rules were known to the employee in the event of a legal action against the company.

Behavioral training is usually conducted either by outside consultants or by using complete programs developed by outsiders. Except for very large companies, resources are not usually available to develop this kind of material in-house.

Other Sources of Training

A number of communities have courses available that meet special needs. While it is probably too costly and impractical to send an entire staff for outside training, specialized courses, such as a wine course or a class on supervision or merchandising, can supplement in-house programs for specialized jobs.

In larger cities, some trade unions offer a selection of classes for their members. The National Restaurant Association and some of the state restaurant associations also give seminars from time to time, as do community colleges with hotel and restaurant programs.

Some off-premise programs contain a "train-the-trainer" element. The material is designed to instruct managers and supervisors, who then take the program back and conduct it themselves in their own departments. This kind of program is highly cost effective in that it expands the number of employees who benefit from the cost of one registration. In addition, the material, although professionally developed, can be customized by the manager for his particular group of employees, and it can be presented at times most convenient for the work schedule of the department. Furthermore, the sessions can be repeated for new employees or reviewed from time to time with all employees.

For some subject material, outside consultants or specialists can be employed to conduct in-house programs. A wine consultant can be brought in to conduct training in wine service, for example. However, unless the individual can be reengaged periodically, it is not possible to repeat the program.

Reinforcing Training

If training is not reinforced on the job, the effort has been wasted, and the investment in materials, trainers, outside consultants, training equipment, and training time will have produced no return.

When employees have been trained to use certain techniques or to do things a certain way, but they do not perform as trained, it may mean that they think it really does not matter. Some reinforcement is needed.

Reinforcement techniques include brief reminders at daily lineups, periodic staff meetings at which techniques and policies are reviewed, role plays of specific situations, or visits from outside experts. Perhaps the strongest reinforcement of all is the model that supervisors and managers present by their own behavior. When supervisors serve an item incorrectly or use poor interpersonal techniques with a guest, the message is broadcast that the training was not important and can be ignored.

HIRING NEW EMPLOYEES— RECRUITING SOURCES

We said earlier that one of the requirements of a successful training program was a motivated trainee. Where do you find motivated trainees? The hiring process is a critical step in the development of an effective, productive staff.

The sources used to recruit new employees will vary depending on the local labor market and the type of employee sought. Typical sources are:

- Advertisements in newspapers
- Advertisements in specialized media, such as local restaurant journals and newsletters
- Private agencies
- Government agencies
- Student placement services at schools
- Referrals from present employees
- Union hiring halls
- Walk-ins

There are advantages and disadvantages to each of these sources. Advertisements in daily or weekly newspapers reach a wide readership at relatively low cost. The disadvantage is that they often produce a large number of applicants, many of whom will not be suited for the job. Unless the company has a personnel officer who can do prescreening, managers and supervisors may have to spend considerable time interviewing and screening candidates.

Private agencies require a fee, which can be quite high. They do perform a screening function, however. Because of the economics involved, agencies are not a usual source of hourly personnel but may be used to hire skilled or supervisory-level candidates.

Government agencies do not charge a fee, but the caliber of

applicants supplied by state agencies is usually not very high. Student placement offices in schools and colleges may be a very good source for recruiting certain positions. There is usually no fee involved. The difficulty with student labor is that it tends to be seasonal; that is, students want to work during the school year and take time off for exams and vacations.

Many employers say their best source for recruitment is their own employees. In fact, for most positions it may be their only source. The applicant has already been prescreened by the referring employee. There is no cost involved, and there is a high probability that the new person will work out because the referring employee has an interest in seeing that he does.

Unions

In some unionized companies, jobs must be posted with the unions. However, there is no requirement that a union candidate be hired. For operations that prefer to hire experienced and trained waiters, the union is a good source. The problem is that at any given time, the pool of waiters looking for jobs usually contains a high proportion of poorer workers; the better ones are already employed.

Walk-ins

Occasionally a job applicant will walk in off the street on the chance that the restaurant may be hiring. Walk-ins are usually seeking unskilled jobs. Generally, most managers consider walk-ins a poor source for desirable workers.

HIRING PROCEDURES

All candidates should be required to complete an application for employment. This need not be a complicated form but should include certain pertinent information: name and address, telephone number, social security number, past employment history, education, and references.

The candidate should then be interviewed to determine his

general suitability for employment. This preliminary interview may be conducted by someone other than the supervisor or manager. In larger companies it is done by the personnel office. The preliminary interview should establish evidence of the candidate's stability, as indicated by length of time at present address and length of time in previous job, and a reasonable reason for leaving his previous employer. The interviewer should also establish the type of work the candidate is seeking, the salary range, and the working hours. He should review the information on the application blank for legibility, completeness, and accuracy. He should look for evidence that the applicant is able to work with other people and take direction and that he appears to have a state of health adequate for the job. If the candidate meets these preliminary requirements and the job opening is what he is seeking, he is then scheduled for a second interview with the department supervisor. In this second interview, the supervisor examines the candidate's qualifications for the specific job opening.

Typical job requirements for service personnel are a clean, neat, and pleasant appearance; an alert, courteous attitude; a calm temperament and even disposition; and the ability to read and speak English and do simple arithmetic computations. The candidate must be able to stand for long periods of time and to carry heavy trays. In operations serving alcoholic beverages, the applicant must meet minimum standards required by state liquor laws.

In addition, the supervisor will ask the applicant about his previous work experience to establish the type of jobs held previously, reasons for leaving, and what the applicant liked and disliked about his previous positions. Answers to this type of question can indicate how the person will adapt to the new work situation.

If the candidate meets the job qualifications, he may be hired pending a reference check and a physical examination. References should be checked regardless of how promising the applicant may appear. The check should include the applicant's last employer, but only if the applicant is no longer working for him. A current employer should be contacted only if the applicant gives his consent.

Personnel officers usually prefer to make reference checks by telephone. The information can be obtained quickly and follow-up questions can be asked. Another advantage to the telephone check is that people will say things on the phone that they would not put in writing. Their tone of voice can also provide clues, which can be followed up with further questions.

HIRING STANDARDS AND THE LAW

Title VII of the Civil Rights Act of 1964 and the Equal Employment Opportunity Act of 1972 prohibit discrimination of job applicants. These statutes make it unlawful for an employer to "fail or refuse to hire or to discharge any individual or otherwise discriminate against any individual" on the basis of race, color, religion, sex, or national origin.

These statutes have considerable implications for hiring in restaurants. The Equal Employment Opportunity Commission (EEOC), which administers these statutes, takes a very narrow view of what constitutes a "bona fide occupational qualification." This means that any requirement that may bar employment to members of a discriminated class (for example, blacks or women) must be proven to be "necessary to the normal operation" of the business. Thus a claim by a luxury restaurant that "female waiters would not be accepted by the guests" is not a valid defense in support of a job requirement that the service staff be male. In a continental restaurant, however, requiring captains to speak fluent French and to have a good working knowledge of French wines and cuisine would be considered a bona fide occupational qualification. Even when a skilled requirement is valid, an employer may still be guilty of discrimination if prevailing conditions were such that a discriminated class was prevented from acquiring the necessary skills for reasons of race, sex, color, religion, or national origin. The employer may be required to provide training to members of a discriminated class and to meet predetermined quotas for the skilled jobs in future hiring.

In 1977 a suit was brought against a group of luxury restaurants in New York City to require them to employ women as waitresses and captains. The suit claimed that sex was not a bona fide occupational qualification. Some of the restaurants named in the suit settled by agreeing to employ a certain percentage of women in these positions within a prescribed time. A number of the restaurants claimed, however, that there were an insufficient number of women qualified for the positions. Several volunteered to provide training for any serious applicant.

The 1967 Age Discrimination in Employment Act and its amendment were mentioned in chapter 8. This act, an amendment to the Fair Labor Standards Act, protects workers between the ages of forty and seventy from arbitrary discrimination based on age.

The Privacy Act of 1974 prevents employers from asking prospective employees certain questions, such as those concerning arrest records or medical conditions. Other areas of questioning that may be seen as discriminatory are also prohibited. These include credit reference checks, marital status, method of birth control, or plans to have children (asked of women only). An interviewer must be prepared to show why his line of inquiry does not discriminate against the prospective employee.

14
The Employee Handbook

(handwritten: what handbook should include)

(handwritten: → employee handbook a contract between employee and employer)

The employee handbook is one way companies communicate standards to their employees. However, it is not just a training medium. The courts have ruled that employee handbooks form an "employment contract," and employers can be legally bound by the provisions of the book.

An employee handbook for service employees should contain three sections: the introduction, general house policies, and specific policies.

The introduction includes some background about the restaurant and why it is special. It may include some of the history of the operation or perhaps something about the founders or owners. If the operation has a theme, the introduction should include some background information about that theme. It should also include the organization's mission statement or operating philosophy. The purpose of the introduction is to instill

(handwritten: → what is purpose of introduction)

pride in the employee, to communicate that he or she is working in a *special* place and is, therefore, a *special* person.

General house policies are the rules and procedures that pertain to all employees. They include:

- Payroll policies and procedures
- Employee benefits
- Employee breaks and meal policies
- Appearance standards and uniform policies
- Work scheduling procedures
- Union grievance procedures and other union-related information
- Causes for dismissal, including policies on theft, substance abuse, and so on
- Other general personnel policies

The third section of the dining room service employee handbook contains specific information about the department and the job. For service personnel, this includes the service standards and procedures that have been discussed in earlier chapters of this book, as well as other policies and procedures that only pertain to dining room operations. This material includes:

- The steps of service: the procedures for taking orders, delivering food and drinks, and clearing tables
- The proper table setting for each meal period and sales outlet
- The details of service: how each menu item is to be served
- Merchandising and selling procedures

It may also include instructions on how to perform specific tasks.

Since the dining room service section of the handbook does not pertain to all employees, and since the details of service can change with each revision of the menu, this section is often produced separately from the main part of the handbook.

The following is a portion of the service section of an employee manual for The Corner, a restaurant in New York's World Trade Center (used by permission of Inhilco).

[handwritten margin notes: "items that pertain to all employees"; "specific job duties discussed"]

Welcome to The Corner!

Our restaurant, like all of the other food facilities in the World Trade Center, is operated by Inhilco, Inc. Our company is a subsidiary of Hilton International.

The Corner is similar in style to a brasserie (an informal French restaurant), but uses American-style menus. The Corner is open from 7 A.M. to 8 P.M. The breakfast menu is in use until 11:30 A.M., at which time The Corner switches to its lunch menu, which is in use for the rest of the day. The assistant manager seats your guests and gives them the menus. You serve them and present the check. The cashier receives the cash. The busboys clean and restock your stations every evening and continually replenish your supplies, clear bus pans and help with the clearing and resetting of tables and counters. Our clientele is largely made up of the business people who work at the World Trade Center. These guests are busy people with limited time for meals.

In order to accommodate our guests, the service in The Corner is fast, yet efficient, and excellent in quality. We expect you to meet our high standards of job performance and, above all, always to be courteous to our guests.

This manual explains all of the tasks you will be required to do. By studying it, and practicing the tasks, you will acquire the skills necessary to perform your job excellently. You will become a professional waitress.

Appearance, Conduct, and Other House Rules

At The Corner, you are visible to the guests at all times. Customers notice the way you look and act, and they form an impression of you. The opinion a customer forms of The Corner is strongly influenced by his opinion of you. By abiding by our policies of appearance and conduct, indicated below, you will leave a lasting positive impression on your customers and you will build a fine reputation for The Corner.

Appearance

You should be impeccably groomed at all times. Your hair should be neat and styled. Pull it back, if it is long, and do not let it fly around, as this is unsanitary. In order to look your best, we require that you wear lipstick, powder, and eye make-up, lightly applied and refreshed before each meal. Jewelry should be kept to a minimum. Only small rings, small earrings and a wristwatch are permitted. Bracelets, necklaces, dangling earrings, or other large jewelry are not allowed. Because we do not want the customer to smell perfume when he is served his food, you are not allowed to wear any fragrances.

The company will provide you with a uniform. However, it is your responsibility to keep it clean and in good condition. Be sure that it fits you properly. In addition to your uniform, you will have to wear a black, conservative shoe, with closed toe and heel, and neutral, sheer stockings, free of runs. The shoes and stockings are not provided by the company.

Conduct

You should always act like you are a professional: alert, efficient, and attentive to your work. Some simple guidelines, listed below, will help you acquire the professional manner that will distinguish you in the eyes of your guests.

1. Be aware of *what* you say. Do not discuss personal matters and do not talk shop within earshot of the customers.
2. Be aware of the *volume* of your voice. Develop the habit of talking in a whisper to fellow employees. Do not shout across the slide to cooks; call the manager if you have any problem. Direct your busboy unobtrusively.
3. Be aware of your posture. Stand straight and look alert. Do not slouch, lean on slide, or place checks on table while writing. Place arms at your side; do not stand with arms folded or hands in pockets. Bend down elegantly.
4. Show the customer that your attention is on your work. Do not stand around in groups, socializing with fellow employees.
5. Confine your eating, drinking, smoking, reading, chewing gum, sitting, etc. to table T4 during your breaks. This conduct is not allowed on the floor.
6. Count tips during your breaks or after work—not while you are on the floor.
7. Arrange your hair and apply make-up before you begin your shift—not while working.

Employee Meals

You are allowed two free meals on your eight-hour shift. You may eat on your break or before or after work, but never during work. Eat only in the employee eating area (at table T4).

Since you will be eating in the front-of-the-house, your professional conduct must be maintained during your breaks. Avoid acting in a manner that suggests a party is going on. Sit in small groups, with both feet under the table, so customers can walk through the aisle easily.

Select your meal from the list of foods allowed to employees. Then list on a meal check *every* item you have selected. Have the manager or assistant manager sign your meal check. When this is done, you may order your food from the cook. (Note: list every item on the meal check, regardless of whether the cook prepares it or you get it yourself. This is important in calculating our food cost accurately.)

Attendance/Lateness

It is absolutely essential to the smooth operation of The Corner that everyone be punctual and have excellent attendance. This is an important requirement of your job. If an emergency or unusual circumstance compels you to be absent or late, notify the manager as far in advance as possible, so arrangements can be made to find a replacement.

Time Cards

Punch your time card at the start and again at the end of your shift. Change clothing before punching in and after punching out. Have a manager initial your time card after you punch out.

Lockers

You will have the use of a personal locker while you are employed here. There is a fee of $2 for the key.

Phone Calls

You are not allowed to make or receive personal phone calls during working hours, except in cases of emergency.

Friends/Visitors

You may not receive friends or visitors in the restaurant during working hours or during your breaks.

Personnel Office

If you feel you have a problem you would like to discuss with Personnel, go to the office or phone for an appointment.

Work Schedule

Stations are rotated on a weekly basis. The schedule is posted two weeks in advance.

How to Serve the Customer

Our customers are the most important part of our business. Their patronage of our stores makes possible the livelihood of every one of us. The sole purpose of all of our work is to serve them.

It is *you* who have direct contact with our guests. This is why the responsibility of making customers for The Corner and keeping them satisfied largely rests on your shoulders.

In addition, fine service will be of personal benefit to you, because it results in higher tips.

SAMPLE TASK DESCRIPTION—HOW TO USE THE ESPRESSO COFFEE MACHINE

The following are examples of task descriptions, which may be included in a training manual. These examples are from an employee manual for The Corner.

Directions for Making One Cup of Espresso

1. Fill strainer with 1 level spoonful of espresso (use brown measuring spoon). Do not pack down.
2. Insert strainer into machine and lock.
3. Set dial at left to "4."
4. Place cup under spigot.

5. Slide small brown handle to left to start machine.
6. Handle will release when coffee is ready to serve.
7. Remove strainer and dump used grounds; rinse.

Directions for Making Two Cups of Espresso

Same as above except

1. Use 1 heaping spoonful—again, do not pack down.
2. Set dial to "6."
3. Use double strainer handle.

Directions for Making Cappuccino

Make espresso as usual and top it with steamed milkfoam.

To make steamed milkfoam, use a large pitcher and pour milk in—a few ounces only. Pull out steam nozzle at extreme left or right and place pitcher under as deep as possible. Turn valve above all the way open carefully, and work nozzle around until you can see it frothing well. Espresso should be placed in a soup mug and served with milk froth and rest of ingredients. It is best not to pour milk froth through spout, but from the top.

Directions for Raising Water to Maximum Level

In the morning, the water level of the espresso machine is checked to be sure it is maximum. You should not make coffee unless the water level is maximum. If the water falls below that level, fill to maximum as follows:

- Press red button on right of front. This starts the pump.
- Turn brown lever to the left until water reaches maximum. Look at the water level while you are adjusting it, so you do not exceed the maximum.
- Release lever and button.

15

Supervising a Unionized Staff

Unions are a fact of life. They are here to stay, and we must live with them. The fact of unions is neither good nor bad. Some unions are better managed than others. Some are more effective than others in protecting the rights of their members. However, no union can take away management's right to manage *unless management itself has bargained away that right*. This is an important point. The practices that union contracts cover deal with certain basic points: economic issues (such as wages and fringe benefits), job security, grievances, and union security. Working conditions and rules may also be covered. All of these are mechanisms to protect the worker from arbitrary and unfair management practices. In fact, union leaders have acknowledged that management invites unionization through poor management practices. Where employees are reasonably paid and secure in their positions, unions have great difficulty in gaining a foothold.

THE SUPERVISOR'S ROLE IN UNIONIZED COMPANIES

The supervisor is the first line of management. It is his job to carry out the terms of the contract, a contract which he probably did not participate in making. It goes without saying that the supervisor must know the terms of the contract to the letter. Not only must he know what the contract does say, he must know what it *does not* say. Anything not expressly prohibited by the contract is permitted (unless prohibited by law or other authority, such as company regulations or policy). Some managements, however, are fearful of taking any action they feel the union might object to. This attitude can severely limit the supervisor in carrying out his responsibilities and can create precedents that may be very damaging in future negotiations.

Just as the supervisor represents management, the union steward represents the union membership—the employees. It is his job to see that the terms of the contract are carried out. Some stewards, especially newly elected ones, can be a pain in the neck, nitpicking about every minor incident, real or imagined. Others can be highly effective in maintaining the morale and enforcing the work rules in the company. The relationship between shop steward and supervisor usually is a matter of individual personalities and the amount of effort each puts forth in building a good working relationship. Even in companies where labor-management relations have a history of bad blood, individuals can establish a good relationship if they feel it is in their best interest to do so.

The supervisor can improve his side of the relationship by recognizing that it is the steward's job to see that the contract is enforced by the members. Of course, in every contract there are areas of interpretation. The steward is entitled to his interpretation, and the supervisor is entitled to his. The supervisor should also remember, though, that supervisors are not infallible, and he should expect the steward to point out his mistakes.

On the other hand, the supervisor should expect the steward to recognize that managing the department is the supervisor's job, and employees are expected to follow his directives. If they disagree with an order, they are still obligated to carry it out. Later they can file a grievance if they wish.

Both the supervisor and the shop steward are working for the same basic goal—that is, long-term profits. Without profits, neither the company nor the employees' jobs will survive.

THE UNION CONTRACT

The parts of the contract that most concern the supervisor are those dealing with hiring terms, scheduling, job classification, and grievance procedures.

Grievances

The contract will probably spell out the steps to be taken in handling a grievance. Generally, it is in the best interest of the company to settle grievances between employee and supervisor on the spot and without delay. The supervisor must handle each case on its own merit based on the facts, not on emotional interpretations, assumptions, or hearsay. Whether the resolution satisfied the employee or not, the complaint and its disposition should be written up in detail in the department log with all relevant facts included. This provides management with information on the matter in case it surfaces again. It also contributes to a history that can be very useful in identifying sources of complaints and possible need for contract revision in future negotiations.

If the supervisor's decision is not satisfactory to the employee, he has the right to take his grievance to higher management. At this point, the union steward usually becomes involved. After hearing the employee's side, the steward may advise him that he has no case, and the matter is closed. If the steward feels the employee has a case, the formal grievance procedure is initiated; the grievance is put in writing and submitted to the next level of management. If the matter reaches the highest level in the company without being satisfactorily resolved, the contract may state that it must go to an impartial arbitrator whose ruling is binding. Since arbitration is costly, the expense is usually shared by the union and the company. Depending on whether or not the company may be affected in the future by precedents set in arbitration, the company will decide whether or not it wants to fight the grievance. If little is at stake, it may rule at a lower level in favor of an employee, reversing the ruling of the first-line supervisor in order to keep the peace. Supervisors should be aware that this may be the outcome of a grievance, and if they are in doubt about making their charges stick, they should check with their superiors first.

Working Hours, Meal Breaks, and Length of Workday

Another part of the contract will deal with such factors as length of workday, premiums for overtime, meal breaks, and allowances for changing of uniforms. It may also specify conditions for days off on weekends and weekdays.

These terms must be considered when scheduling and also when preparing information for payroll. A supervisor may find, however, that the company has inadvertently been paying for things that are not really required by the contract. If the practice has been of short duration, the company stands a good chance of getting it corrected. If the practice has been going on for a long time, the union may consider it a past practice that must be continued even though it is not specified in the contract. Arbitrators have upheld this position in previous cases. If you find a situation like this, you should bring the matter to management's attention before attempting to do anything about it. In the future, beware of setting a precedent that could become a bothersome past practice in the future.

Hiring Terms

A contract may provide for the hiring of new employees on a provisional basis for a certain period of time. During this time, the employment may be terminated for any reason. After the provisional period, the employee may be terminated only for cause. If you do not take action quickly to dismiss a provisional employee whose performance is not satisfactory, you may be stuck with him.

Job Classifications and Descriptions

Most contracts contain a list of job titles and their negotiated wage rates without a detailed description of each job. In table service restaurants, job content is defined by tradition. For an existing restaurant, the job consists of whatever the individual was doing in that job in the past. However, there are gray areas. In one restaurant, it is the busboy's job to vacuum the dining room carpet; in another restaurant, this job is done by a porter. Waitresses in a coffee shop usually draw their own beer; in a table service restaurant, a bartender may draw it for them. In one private club, a captain relieves on the maître d's day off; in another, the manager performs this job. In one restaurant, waiters bus their own tables if they have time and the busboy is busy. In the establishment down the street, waiters would not think of bussing a table. These are some of the gray areas that exist when there are no defined job descriptions.

It is difficult to state generalities in realigning job content; but as a rule, the union is most concerned about maintaining the relative distinctions between skill levels for the jobs and their related wage scales. In the case of vacuuming, there is not much difference between the busboy level and the porter job, except that the busboy is usually considered a tipped employee. If the busboy would receive less in tips as a result of his taking on vacuuming duties, the union could require that he be paid a higher rate for vacuuming time. In the case of waiters bussing tables, the situation is not as clear. If it could be shown that the waiters would serve more customers and therefore increase their income if they bussed tables, they would probably accept such a change in job content. However, if this change meant that the waiter staff would be cut (and therefore produce less revenue for the union in dues and welfare contributions), the union might object.

Skill level is another consideration. Asking higher-paid employees to perform lower-rated jobs, such as asking a waiter or captain to vacuum, would probably produce opposition. In a young, recently opened restaurant, there are no precedents, and management has more freedom in determining job content (unless the new restaurant is one of a chain, in which case precedents have been established in other units). The last defense against rigid job content is having written job descriptions that are general enough to permit flexibility when needed, but still provide a workable description of the job.

In restaurants that are innovative or offer new concepts, there is also less opposition to nonconventional job contents. The more progressive unions are recognizing the need to increase productivity in order to save existing jobs and create new ones. Combination jobs, such as having a bartender serve a limited number of food items at the bar, is a recent development. Under less enlightened conditions, a restaurant wishing to have hot, carved sandwiches at a stand-up bar would have been required to staff the operation with a bartender and a carver, regardless of the volume of business.

Where job content is long established, making changes is difficult, even with union cooperation. It is best to make a number of very small changes to avoid a major upheaval in the operation. It is not easy to change habits and practices that have been in effect for years. Even the smallest change in routine can be very upsetting to some people, especially older employees. The best advice is to move slowly. Sooner or later you will accomplish your goals.

THE SUPERVISOR'S ROLE IN CONTRACT NEGOTIATION

In all probability, you will not be asked to participate in contract negotiations. They are usually handled by top management and labor lawyers. You can, however, play a part in negotiations by making recommendations ahead of time concerning contract terms that are especially bothersome. Some companies have formal planning sessions with supervisors prior to negotiations to solicit this type of information and to get their opinions on contract clauses under consideration. Your department logbook is especially useful in providing specific cases and details.

Union Organizing Drives

If your company is engaged in a union organizing drive, you should be instructed by management as to what you may or may not do. Federal regulations are very explicit about what constitutes an unfair labor practice. You should be very familiar with these regulations so you will not accidentally cause the company to be in violation of the law or jeopardize the company's bargaining position.

Generally, during a union organizing drive, you should do the following:

1. If a union representative approaches you, refer him to the manager in a courteous manner. Do not engage in any conversation or discussion with him. If he approaches employees during working hours or on company property, inform the manager at once. You do not have to permit him access to nonpublic areas of the restaurant.
2. Do not discuss the union drive with the employees. Management will probably state the company's position to all employees at one time. You may jeopardize the company's position by making illegal statements.
3. Do not single out antiunion employees for special favors or prounion employees for disciplinary action, such as dismissal or layoff.

16

Controlling Dining Room Labor Cost

Payroll is by far the largest cost in the operation of a dining room. It includes not only the direct hourly wages of the service staff but also a number of related costs, sometimes referred to as "fringes." These include:

1. The employer's share of social security taxes. (In 1988 this is 7.51 percent of each employee's wages up to a maximum income of $45,000, or a maximum of $3379.50 per employee.)
2. Federal and state unemployment insurance. (Each employer's rate is based on the number of former employees drawing unemployment compensation.)
3. Workman's compensation insurance. (This provides health care for employees injured on the job. The rate varies from state to state.)

   These costs are set by law. In addition, most employers offer some type of paid vacation and sick pay. Many also pay all or part of the cost of health insurance and life insurance. If the staff is unionized, the union contract may require the employer to make contributions to union pension and welfare funds. Such contributions are usually figured on the basis of a set amount per union member or on the basis of manhours worked by union members each month.

Another group of costs directly related to the payroll are employee meals. Most employers provide free meals for their employees during their work shift. The cost of these meals is considered a part of the fringe benefit cost.

These related payroll costs can greatly increase the total payroll. In fact, in unionized companies, related payroll expenses can be as much as one-third of the total payroll or more.

These costs are considered part of total payroll, a cost for which the dining room supervisor is held accountable by management. There are other costs of employing people that are less easily identified but that exist nonetheless. Uniform cost is one. The cost of buying and laundering uniforms is usually not charged against specific departments, and it can be a considerable expense to a restaurant. If the company pays the service staff to maintain their own uniforms, this cost is easily identifiable by department.

Other hidden costs include preparing payroll each week, maintaining the extensive personnel records required by the government, cleaning and maintaining employee locker rooms and lunchroom facilities, and performing various personnel functions—recruiting, training, and so forth.

Fortunately for the dining room manager, service payrolls are among the easiest to control in the restaurant. Most tipped employees prefer not to work if business is slow and their income from tips is down. The day-to-day mechanics of controlling labor costs include the following:

1. Scheduling based on forecasts of sales and standards of productivity.
2. Controlling overtime.
3. Providing proper information for preparing payroll and reviewing payroll reports.

Before effective scheduling can be done, though, two essential management tools must be developed: productivity standards and staffing guides. Other, longer-range tools (including job analysis and work simplification), the selection of productive employees, and a continuing program of training and retraining are also effective in controlling labor cost. Hiring and training were discussed in chapter 13. The final and perhaps most important factor in labor cost control is a motivated, productive staff that works together as a team. Motivation was discussed in chapter 12.

SETTING PRODUCTIVITY STANDARDS

In large companies productivity standards or goals are often set by management. They may be expressed as covers served per manhour or in terms of sales dollars per manhour. If standards have not been established for your operation, you will have to establish your own standards. Since cover counts are easier to use, we will develop the standards on that basis rather than on sales; however, the principle is the same.

Separate standards must be established for each dining room and for each meal period based on the type of service used, the physical layout, the number of seat turnovers, and union contract terms. It is helpful to know what productivity you are now achieving. To get the overall rate, you need the total covers served during an average week and the number of hours worked by the service department for that week. The following formula is used:

$$\frac{\text{Total covers served}}{\text{Total hours worked}} = \text{Covers per manhour}$$

This computation provides a general measure of productivity. Now take it further and break it down by the various meal periods using the same basic formula.

$$\frac{\text{Total breakfast covers served}}{\text{Total hours worked for breakfast}} = \frac{\text{Covers per manhour}}{\text{for breakfast}}$$

In making your analysis, use a test period of at least one week and choose a time when there are no unusual operating conditions that would distort the result, such as holidays or bad weather. Set up your results in a table like that shown in figure 16-1. (Figures 16-1 through 16-8 will be used as examples throughout this discussion.) From this illustration you can quickly see which time periods have the lowest productivity and are pulling down your average. These periods should be examined first, although you will probably want to look at all segments of the operation to do a thorough analysis.

For each meal period, go back and figure the productivity day by day and set those results in a table. Look at the days that had the highest productivity. On those particular days, was the staff pushed? Did service suffer? It is not good to set standards at peak levels.

People can extend themselves for short periods of time when they have to but should not be expected to operate at that level all the time. Also, the object is not to cut back the level of service from our defined standards but rather to have sufficient staff on hand to provide that level at all times without overstaffing. Look also at the days with the lowest productivity levels. Were these times when you had the same amount of staff, but business was off? If you find that certain days of the week have particularly low productivity you have already identified areas

	Average Covers	Waiter Hours Scheduled	Covers per Hour
Breakfast 6–11 AM	520	48	10.8
Lunch 11–2 PM	450	36	12.5
Afternoon 2–5 PM	175	12	14.6
Dinner 5–10 PM	435	46	9.5
Late Supper 10–1 AM	125	12	10.4
Total	1705	154	11.1

16-1. Waiter productivity by meal period.

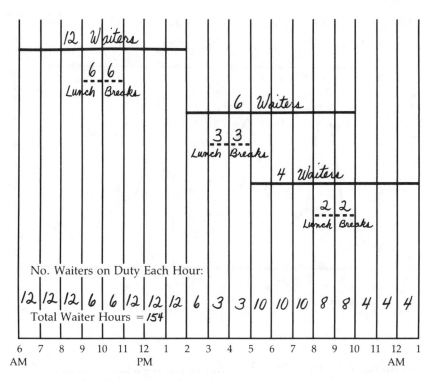

16-2. Original staffing chart.

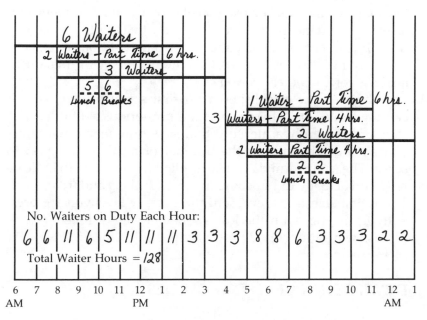

16-3. Revised staffing chart.

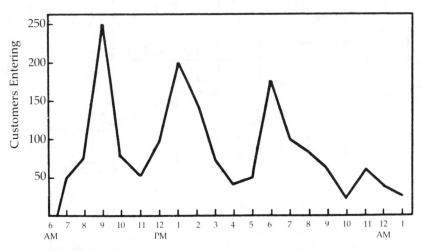

16-4. Typical hourly flow of business: number of customers arriving each hour.

for improvement in scheduling. You may also find some days with very high productivity caused by short staffing or an unusual influx of business. If you find any days with productivity too high to maintain or excessively low, eliminate them and take as your standard the average productivity of the remaining days. If weekend business patterns are different from weekdays, you may need to set a separate standard for them. Make this analysis for each meal period.

You have now established your first set of productivity or staffing standards. There is nothing mysterious about them. A standard is simply a measure that says how many manhours you should schedule for the number of meals you expect to serve. The same formula can be applied to the result to indicate how you actually did in comparison with the standard or goal. These first standards represent the average level you are presently achieving, with the low spots eliminated. Later we will discuss ways to increase productivity still further.

DEVELOPING STAFFING GUIDES

The productivity standard is a tool for figuring out how many manhours the business will require for each meal period. The

Time Period	Covers	Staffing—Original	Productivity (Covers per Waiter Hour)
6–7 AM	40	12	6.6 *
7–8	90	12	7.5
8–9	250	12	20.8
9–10	80	6	13.3
10–11	60	6	10.0
11–12	100	12	8.3
12–1 PM	200	12	16.7
1–2	150	12	12.5
2–3	75	6	12.5
3–4	40	3	13.3
4–5	60	3	20.0
5–6	175	10	17.5
6–7	100	10	10.0
7–8	80	10	8.0
8–9	60	8	7.5
9–10	20	8	2.5
10–11	60	4	15.0
11–12	40	4	10.0
12–1 AM	25	4	6.25
Total or Average	1705	154	11.1
*For First Half Hour of Service			

16-5. Productivity by hour.

	Average Covers	Waiter Hours Scheduled	Covers per Hour
Breakfast 6–11 AM	520	34	15.3
Lunch 11–2 PM	450	33	13.6
Afternoon 2–5 PM	175	9	19.4
Dinner 5–10 PM	435	28	15.5
Late Supper 10–1 AM	125	7	17.8
Total	1705	111	15.4

16-6. Waiter productivity with revised schedule (for weekdays only).

staffing guide shows how those hours should be scheduled in order to meet the demands of service without having unproductive labor. Staffing guides are shown in figures 16-2 and 16-3. Each person's hours are plotted by half hour, and the lunch breaks are also shown. The number of people on duty in each half-hour segment can then be quickly seen and compared to the flow of business in the same half-hour segment. Figure 16-4 shows a typical pattern. You should determine your own pattern during a test period. When you add the amount of time required on each shift for setup and clean up, the staffing guide tells you when you have slack time and when your coverage is thin. Generally, a staffing guide is prepared for the median or average level of business. To provide flexibility for varying levels of business (since manhours are budgeted on the basis of forecasts), the chart may show that certain shifts can be eliminated at low levels of business or added only for peak forecasts.

When the hours of staffing are plotted on a staffing guide, the result usually shows a need for staggered shifts. This is what happened in the example. The entire staff was not needed for setup in the morning and is only present when the peak of business is reached. Since some come in later, they leave later and provide afternoon coverage. (The original staffing guide showed considerable slack time in the off-peak hours.) When waiters work in teams, staggered shifts are often a very effective scheduling method; one member of the team opens the station

Time Period	Covers	Staffing— Original	Productivity (Covers per Waiter Hour)	Staffing— Revised	Productivity
6–7 AM	40	12	6.6*	6	13.3*
7–8	90	12	7.5	6	15.0
8–9	250	12	20.8	11	22.7
9–10	80	6	13.3	6	13.3
10–11	60	6	10.0	5	12.0
11–12	100	12	8.3	11	9.1
12–1 PM	200	12	16.7	11	18.2
1–2	150	12	12.5	11	13.6
2–3	75	6	12.5	3	25.0
3–4	40	3	13.3	3	13.3
4–5	60	3	20.0	3	20.0
5–6	175	10	17.5	8	21.9
6–7	100	10	10.0	8	12.5
7–8	80	10	8.0	6	13.3
8–9	60	8	7.5	3	20.0
9–10	20	8	2.5	3	6.7
10–11	60	4	15.0	3	20.0
11–12	40	4	10.0	2	20.0
12–1 AM	25	4	6.25	2	12.5
Total or Average	1705	154	11.1	111	15.4

*For First Half Hour of Service

16-7. Productivity by hour revised.

		Mon	Tues	Wed	Thu	Fri	Sat
Breakfast	6:30AM–11AM	545	532	545	528	450	226
Lunch	11–2 PM	436	427	445	463	479	483
Afternoon	2–5 PM	140	164	186	194	191	243
Dinner	5–10 PM	417	429	445	437	447	342
Late Supper	10–1 AM	80	100	125	150	170	221
Total		1618	1652	1746	1772	1737	1515

16-8. Cover counts by day of the week.

and the other closes. This provides continuity of service to the guest at the close of the meal period without holding waiters overtime.

Once you have plotted the shifts, you may find you can cut some slack time off the ends of the shifts and make a significant improvement in overall productivity without sacrificing the level of service during the actual serving period. If this is the case, you should go back and reevaluate your productivity standards in light of the revised staffing guides.

FORECASTING THE BUSINESS AND SCHEDULING FOR THE WEEK

Now you have the basic tools for staffing your dining room effectively. The first step in planning the weekly schedule is forecasting the amount of business that will be done each day for each meal period. In many restaurants, forecasts are regularly prepared by the manager; in others, they are made jointly by the dining room manager, chef, catering manager, and other department heads. If forecasts are not made in your operation, you must make your own. While it sounds difficult and impractical, forecasting skills can be developed with a little practice. First, you need to develop the sales history. If no records are kept of the number of covers served, you will have to start developing your own history. Your manager's logbook is a good tool if you enter the number of covers served at each meal as well as any events of the day that may have influenced the business, such as weather conditions, conventions in town, large parties, special local events (such as athletic events), and so forth. As you build this history, you will notice a pattern forming. Generally, two or three weeks' history is enough to start with, although a longer history is preferred. For holidays, of course, you would need to know what the pattern was last year.

Once you have some history, try to forecast the number of covers for the coming week. Check out the special events planned in the community, conventions, and so forth and use the past two or three weeks as a guideline. Then during the coming week, compare your estimate with the business you actually did. If you are within 5 percent of your forecast, you have done very well. There will be days when an unexpected event, such as a bad storm, will throw the count off. Since you do not staff a business for unexpected occurrences, it is best to label such a day in the history logbook as a fluke and discount it in future forecasts. Do not let such days prevent you from carrying on with your forecasts.

SCHEDULING: COMPUTING THE HOURS

With forecasts for each meal period, you are ready to compute the number of waiter hours needed to service the forecasted business in the coming week. This is a simple calculation, dividing the total covers forecast for each meal period by the productivity goal for that period. If 300 covers are forecast for Monday lunch and the standard is 25 lunch covers per waiter, then $300 \div 25 = 12$ waiters required for Monday lunch. You can save time every week by setting up a little chart for yourself for the various levels of business you may experience for each meal period.

Lunch Staffing

Covers	Waiters
200	8
225	9
250	10
275	11
300	12

When you have the number of waiters required, all that remains is to identify the shifts on the staffing chart that are to be filled for the day and assign the members of the staff to the various shifts.

THE EXAMPLE RESTAURANT

Examine figures 16-2 and 16-3 again. These staffing charts are for The Example, a moderately priced 175-seat restaurant in a downtown area. It is open from 6:30 A.M. to 1:00 A.M., Monday through Saturday. The original weekday staffing is as follows:

Early shift 6:00 A.M. to 2:00 P.M.: twelve waiters and waitresses
Middle shift 2:00 P.M. to 10:00 P.M.: six waiters and waitresses
Late shift 5:00 P.M. to 1:00 A.M.: four waiters and waitresses

Everyone gets a one-hour meal break and works a seven-hour day. This schedule requires 154 waiter-hours a day.

During a typical week, The Example serves 10,040 covers with an overall waiter productivity of 10.9 covers per waiter-hour (fig. 16-8). When Saturday activity is excluded, productivity is slightly higher (11.1). These figures indicate that Saturday productivity is lower than the average and is pulling down the overall waiter productivity. The largest volume of business is done during the week, however, and affords a greater potential for savings.

In figure 16-1 the Monday through Friday activity is broken down by meal period. Lunch-time productivity is higher than the overall average, but dinner is below average. The highest productivity is achieved in the afternoon but on a very low volume of business.

The manager of The Example plotted the flow of business by hour (fig. 16-4). This showed him where the business peaked. He also charted his staffing (fig. 16-2) and computed the productivity hour-by-hour (fig. 16-5). This showed him what he was achieving at peak periods and where the slack was in the schedule.

Now he began to develop his staffing standards by determining the coverage he needed to service the peak periods. There were at maximum 12 stations in the 175-seat dining room. The manager estimated that at lunch time people were seated, ate, and left in thirty minutes or less during the 12 noon to 1:00 P.M. period. Since parties of 3 are seated at tables for 4 and single guests are seated at deuces, it is unlikely that a waiter would have all of his seats occupied at any given time. Therefore, he assumed that only 75 to 80 percent of the chairs are occupied even when the restaurant is at full capacity. Thus the most a waiter could attain on a 16-seat station during the hour would be two sittings of 12 people or 24 covers. This figure represents an absolute maximum. It assumes that there is a waiting line and that whenever a table is vacated, another party is waiting to sit down. It also assumes that people are able to be served as quickly as they wish with no slowdowns or delays in service.

Using 24 covers per station or per waiter per hour, the manager estimated he could serve a maximum of 280 people in the peak lunch hour. In other words, for every 24 covers served in that hour, he needed one more waiter. This analysis shows that, for the week he studied, he only needed 8 waiters instead of 12 since he served an average of 200 people, not 280.

But there is a catch. With only 8 waiters, he would have to either close down 4 stations, assign 22-seat stations, or do a combination of the two. Now what happens if the 200 guests do not arrive at even intervals and the dining room does not turn over according to plan? What would happen if three-quarters of them arrive at the beginning of the hour? If you are operating with reduced seating, you force 50 people to stand in line for a half hour, which would upset many guests on short lunch breaks. Or you could fill those big 22-seat stations and take the risk that some of the waiters will get stuck and give slow service. Between 8 and 12 waiters are needed for this situation. The manager decided to try it with 10.

Next, the manager examined the breakfast service. Here he assumed only a 60 percent utilization of seats since there are more single people and parties of 2 at breakfast than there are at lunch. He also used a maximum of 2.5 sittings per hour. This produced a maximum of approximately 260 people during the peak hour, very close to the 250 average during the week he analyzed (fig. 16-4). With lower seat utilization, however, the manager felt the waiters could handle larger stations at breakfast than they could at lunch, and he decided to try working breakfast with 11 waiters instead of 12. Using the same method, he determined that dinner service required 8.

Finally, there are periods when a minimum staffing is required, regardless of the volume of business. For late supper, the manager wanted a minimum of two waiters on duty until closing. He also wanted at least three until 11:00 P.M. since the late supper business was somewhat unpredictable. By 11:00 P.M., however, they could usually tell what the rest of the evening's business would be like. If it looked like a rush, the third person could stay on another hour.

Now the manager had his peak hour requirements for breakfast, lunch, and dinner. Unfortunately, we cannot schedule workers only for the hour we need them; we must give them enough work to make it worth their while to come in. In fact, most union contracts require that a worker be paid for a minimum number of hours (usually four if he reports to work as scheduled). Therefore, the staffing required at peak times at least partially determines the staffing of off-peak periods. We can utilize off-peak times for meal breaks and sidework, and we can employ part-timers for some of the time slots. Usually, though, it is difficult to find waiters to work only breakfast since tips are lower than at other meals. Most waiters want to work lunch as well to make their tips. Therefore, the manager at The Example had to revise his figures for lunch and schedule 11 waiters in order to have 11 for breakfast coverage. Now he charted his revised schedule and recalculated the productivity for each hour. In the periods where productivity was low, he tried staggering the shifts and substituting part-time help until he brought each time slot to an acceptable level. The final result is shown in figures 16-3, 16-6, and 16-7.

The revised schedule required 111 manhours as opposed to 154 required by the original schedule, a 28 percent reduction and an increase of productivity from 11.1 to 15.4. The largest increase was in late supper productivity, which rose from 10.4 to 17.8. This figure is a bit misleading, however, since the manager had provided himself with contingency coverage in case he needed it. The old schedule had been planned to cover higher levels of business even though they may not materialize. The new schedule provides flexibility. The gains in other periods were more concrete, however. Dinner increased from 9.5 to 15.5, a gain of 6 covers per man-hour. Breakfast showed a gain of 4.5 covers. These rates of productivity represent reasonable, attainable standards for the restaurant.

We can take this analysis one step further. These productivity rates were established on the basis of an average. Averages are combinations of low values and high values. The covers served by day of the week are shown in figure 16-8. Generally, the counts are quite consistent. However, several are out of line. Friday breakfast, for example, is quite a bit lower than the rest of the week. If this is a regular occurrence, our standard reflects lower productivity for that meal period. On Monday, business also seems to slacken after lunch. For late supper there is a wide range between the lowest day and the highest. Saturday, which we have not considered so far, shows a very different pattern of business. Separate standards could be set up for Saturday, using the same methodology the manager applied in developing his weekday schedule and standards.

INCREASING PRODUCTIVITY

It may be possible to make even greater improvement in the productivity and reduce labor costs further by looking at job content and applying job analysis—that is, analyze starting times and flow of business and possibly alter the reservation policy. Here are some techniques that payroll consultants use:

1. Make spot observations of the staff at selected times before, during, and after service. Note how much time is really spent productively and how much is idle. Adjust schedules accordingly. Job analysis and work simplification will be discussed later.
2. Check your hours of operation. Perhaps you can close earlier or open later without significant loss of business. Of course, operating hours are a management decision that must take into consideration all activities of the business, not only the dining room staffing.
3. Using the hourly flow of business (discussed in relation to the staffing guide), look at the troughs or slow periods to see where you could build sales volume by special promotions. Increasing sales does wonders for productivity and for the bottom line of the income statement.
4. If you have a reservations policy, review it in terms of your seating patterns and turnover. One luncheon club was able to get a partial second sitting, which is unheard of in that type of operation. They achieved it by using a no-reservations policy. This forced members to come before 12:15 to be sure of getting a table, instead of 12:30 or 1:00, which is the usual time in this city. Members soon discovered that if they could not get to the dining room by 12:15, they could always get a seat around 1:30. As a result, the service hours were spread out and the number of covers a waiter could serve in a lunch period were increased. On the other hand, Windows On The World in New York is able to achieve two full turnovers a night by forcing reservations into two seatings. Reservations are accepted for seating between 5:00 and 6:30 and from 9:00 to 10:30. No reservations are accepted for the 6:30 to 9:00 period because the dining room is full during that time. A few walk-ins and late reservations may be sandwiched in if the first sitting vacates in time; otherwise, it is reservations only from 9:00 P.M. on.

CONTROLLING OVERTIME

One area that can be very costly if not controlled is overtime. Companies that carefully control labor costs usually require some type of prior approval by management before overtime can be paid. Such policies must be well publicized to the staff. The employees must be aware that they cannot just set their own working hours and expect to be paid for them. Some favorite tactics are punching in an hour or two early, then taking an extra meal break or spending the time puttering about the dining room, setting up at a leisurely pace. At the end of the shift there are still guests on the station who must be served or sidework to be done, and suddenly overtime is necessary. Another trick is to delay and putter with closing duties, necessitating an extra hour or two to finish up. If these practices are allowed to continue, they suddenly become built in. There may be situations where overtime is unavoidable, as with banquets that break up later than scheduled. There may also be scheduling situations when an extra hour or two is really needed at the end of a shift. It may be less costly to pay the overtime premium than to bring in an extra person to cover. However, this is a decision the supervisor must make as part of his scheduling process, and must not be the prerogative of the employee.

PAYROLL PREPARATION

The last step in day-to-day labor cost control is proper preparation of payroll information. It is the responsibility of the dining room supervisor to see that the correct number of hours worked are reported to the payroll department. If meal breaks are not paid time, they must be subtracted from the hours worked. The company should also have a policy on docking for lateness. Finally, the supervisor should review the payroll after it is prepared to see that each person was paid for the correct amount of hours and at the proper rate. Employees are quick to tell you if they were underpaid but not so quick to report on overpayment.

WORK SIMPLIFICATION AND JOB ANALYSIS

Work simplification (the old time-and-motion study idea) is being used more and more in restaurants to improve productivity. While it is more applicable in kitchen and dishroom areas, it still may be a useful technique in improving the efficiency in some dining room functions.

Serving guests at tables is largely a matter of gathering items and carrying them either directly to the table or to a nearby service station. Some time may be saved by (1) shortening the distance to be traveled, (2) reducing the number of trips necessary (although your success in carrying out this suggestion will often depend on when the guests are ready for their next course), and (3) reducing the amount of time required to gather the items in the kitchen.

Industrial engineers use the technique of job analysis. First, they break down each task into its most basic components. These are usually classified according to the following categories:

1. Operation (for example, dip soup)
2. Inspection
3. Transportation
4. Delay or wait

Since transporting time and waiting add nothing to the value of the item, the objective is to reduce the time spent in these functions. For example, you cannot eliminate a flight of stairs between the kitchen and the dining room, but you can cut down on the number of trips to the kitchen. Relocating coffee, rolls, salads, and desserts to a service pantry near the dining room would reduce the number of trips made to the kitchen. A communications system or electronic cash register point-of-sale computer terminal to transmit orders to the kitchen would eliminate other trips. Waits at the range for hot food would be eliminated by a signal device that would tell the waiter when his order is ready.

Storing equipment and supplies close to the point of use also reduces walking time. You may want to consider increasing the capacity of dining room side stands and organizing them to permit storage of all ware and supplies needed for a meal period. This would eliminate trips to the kitchen for refills during service. Often the space is there; it is only a matter of organizing it properly. Another time-and-motion technique is to store items that are used together in the same location. The beverage station should be set up with all the items needed for the service of beverages. If iced teaspoons are located next to the iced tea (along with ice, glasses, lemons, and underliners), the waiter will not have to make a separate trip to a side stand to pick them up.

Determine the quantities required for a day or a meal period and set up a standard supply schedule. Organize sidework and busboy duties so that these supplies get to the proper place before service. Avoid multiplication of the same function. Instead of having each captain send a waiter to the storeroom for the team's condiment and matches supplies, send one person for the entire department.

Another idea is to put things on wheels. Setup time can be reduced by wheeling dish dollies and glass racks into the dining room. One team sets the placemats and napkins for the entire room. A second team sets the silver, working off a cart that is rolled down the room. The third team sets the coffee cups and water glasses, working directly from the glass racks and dish dollies. This assembly line method cuts the setup time in half and is preferable to the old method in which each server has to make several trips to the kitchen, hunting down the equipment he needs and hand carrying it to his tables.

Another approach to work simplification involves asking the following questions about each task:

1. What is the task to be done?
2. Why is it really necessary?
3. When should it be done?
4. Who should do it?
5. How should it be done?

One supervisor asked, "Why is it necessary to vacuum the dining room carpet twice a day?" He purchased a carpet sweeper to use after lunch where needed and saved three-quarters of an hour. The carpet is vacuumed after lunch only if it is really needed.

In another restaurant, waitresses were spending too much

time waiting for their toast to pop out of two small toasters. The supervisor requested installation of a larger rotary toaster. It was faster and had a larger capacity. When a waitress needed toast, she put two slices in and took the next two slices that came out. Although there was an occasional wasted slice, waiting time and stress were greatly reduced.

In an ice cream parlor, waitresses made their own sundaes and sodas. On a busy day this took a great deal of time away from their stations and caused considerable congestion and delay at the fountain. The supervisor assigned one person to be the soda jerk and was able to reduce the service staff by two waitresses—a net reduction of one person.

For many tasks, a single improvement made after applying work simplification techniques may not seem significant. However, when all of the various tasks are put together, there can be a visible improvement in the overall productivity of the department.

17
Cashiering and Revenue Control

There are two ways of collecting cash in table service restaurants. The customer either makes his payment directly to a cashier, or he pays the waiter (who then settles with the cashier). A variation of this second method is to have the waiter maintain his own bank and settle with the cashier (or manager) once at the end of the shift. This procedure is used in some counter service operations where each counter has its own cash register, and in some cocktail lounges and restaurants as well.

In large restaurants, the dining room supervisor is not usually responsible for cashiering. In small operations, especially fast-turnover restaurants where the customer pays the cashier directly, the supervisor may be responsible for the cashiering function.

Whatever system is used, whether or not the dining room supervisor is responsible for the actual collection of the revenue, he *is* responsible for seeing that his staff charges correctly for the items they serve, that all money collected is turned in to the cashier, that customers are not overcharged or otherwise cheated, and that customers do not walk out without paying.

COMMON CONTROL SYSTEMS IN TABLE SERVICE RESTAURANTS

In the old hotel system, checkers were stationed in the kitchen. Guests' orders were written down on an order pad. This order was then taken to the checker who assigned a guest check to the waiter and wrote out the order again on his hard check. The checker then entered the prices on the check either by hand or by machine. When the waiter assembled his order, he took it to the cashier station. There, the checker lifted all the lids and inspected the tray to be sure all items were listed on the check. When the guest was ready to settle the check, the checker totaled it and prepared a detailed record of the check and the charges. The waiter then collected cash from the guest (or had the check signed for a charge) and turned in the check and cash collected to a cashier who completed the transaction. At the end of the meal, the cashier's records had to match the checker's records. If a check was missing, the waiter was held responsible for the amount as recorded by the checker.

The rising cost of labor made the checker system practically obsolete. Checking was more often done on a test basis by managers, captains, or controller's representatives using the precheck system. Here, the waiter is assigned a number of guest checks. When he takes an order, he records the items on the check. He then takes it to a precheck machine where he enters the prices and totals. This priced check is presented to the barman or chef to obtain food or drinks. These individuals will not give out any food or beverage that has not been rung up on the check. A variation of this system uses a machine with a throwcheck or ticket that is turned in instead of the check. Some checks have duplicate copies or stubs that are submitted in place of the check itself.

When the guest pays, the waiter takes the check and cash

(or charge) payment to a cashier station where the transaction is rung up on a cash register. The cashier rings the amounts for food, beverages, tax, and other charges on the back of the check.

At the end of the day, the amounts entered on the precheck machine should match the amount of cash and charges collected, as shown on the cashier's register.

The key points in these control systems are as follows:

1. Control of guest checks. Waiters cannot present a check to a guest for payment and then pocket the money and destroy the check. All checks must be numbered consecutively and be accounted for (including reserve stocks).
2. Control of merchandise issues. Main entrée and drink charges must be entered on the guest check before the waiter can pick up the items. This control is not usually extended to appetizers, desserts, and other lesser valued items, although it may be if necessary.
3. Comparison of merchandise issued from the kitchen (according to the chef's records) with the sales recorded on guests' checks.
4. Comparison of guest check totals with detail tapes in registers. This would be done on a test basis only, or if a discrepancy were found.
5. Comparison of the dining room manager's cover count with the total number of covers on guest checks.

With electronic point-of-sale equipment, a prechecking system can provide even more control and information than a mechanical system. A computer system can provide reports of sales by item for matching with the kitchen and bar records; stubs or tickets for any menu item, printed remotely at the proper station in the kitchen; and control over guest checks which are not printed or numbered until they are used. With some systems, there is no check at all until the computer prints it out. (See fig. 17-3.)

In fast-service restaurants with low average checks, the cost of an elaborate prechecking system is usually not warranted. An additional consideration is speed. Such an operation depends on fast turnover of seats to offset low checks. Therefore, any control system used should not slow down service. In this type of operation, controls still require accounting for checks and may include comparison of kitchen production against sales on checks. Other aspects of control usually require direct, on-the-spot supervision. Waiters should be required to price out their checks and leave them on the table or counter when the main course is served. Room supervisors can look to see that checks are properly made out and include all items that have been served to that table.

CASHIERING PROCEDURES

Cashiers must be impressed with the importance of following proper procedures in handling money and the need for arithmetic accuracy in preparing their reports. They should be required to sign a statement to the effect that any funds assigned to them are the property of the company and that they will bear full responsibility for all overages and shortages. State labor laws vary on the employer's right to make employees pay the amount of a shortage. But even if the employee cannot be forced to pay, such a statement still has psychological value. In addition, all employees who handle cash should be bonded.

Cashiering procedures should be written out in detail and should be available at every cashier station. New employees should be thoroughly trained in these procedures and required to follow them at all times. Listed below are some general procedures that may be used as guidelines. Detailed procedures will vary, depending on the type of operation and the register equipment used.

1. Prior to opening for business, the cashier should count the bank to confirm that the correct amount of money is there. As a rule, a cashier's bank is maintained at the same amount, and the cashier is required to sign for this amount when it is initially issued. If the amount of the bank is changed, the cashier should be required to sign a new receipt showing the amount of the revised bank.
2. The cashier station should be kept orderly at all times. All

bills and coins should be put into the correct sections of the cash drawer.

3. When a customer presents a check and money for payment, the cashier should verbally acknowledge the amount of the check and the amount of money rendered. He should examine the bills carefully, especially those of large denomination, and comment if there are any unusual markings on a bill. It may be a setup for a short-change artist, or the bills may be counterfeit. Any unusual transaction should be referred to the manager or supervisor.

4. The cashier then places the bill on the cash register slab. He inserts the check into the register slot and rings up the amount of the sale according to the instructions for his type of register. If both cash and charge sales are handled, the register will have separate keys for the two types of transactions. Electronic equipment may have a separate key for each type of credit card accepted. It may also compute the amount of change to be returned.

5. The cashier should always count the change twice, once as he removes it from the register and once as he hands it to the customer. If the register does not compute the amount of change to be given, the cashier should start with the amount of the check and then count up to the amount of cash rendered.

6. When the transaction is completed, the customer's money is then placed in the proper section in the register and the drawer is closed. The guest check is removed from the register slot and put in a check box or rack (usually with separate slots for each waiter).

7. Under no circumstances should the cashier leave his station without locking the register. Furthermore, he should keep the drawer shut when not putting money in or taking it out. If a coin falls on the floor, he should give the customer another coin from the cash drawer and look for the lost coin later.

8. The cashier should look at each customer directly when handling the transaction. Eye contact can put off a potential thief because he may think the cashier suspects his intent and is memorizing his appearance.

9. The cashier should complete one transaction at a time and

not permit customers or others to interrupt. A typical tactic of the short-change artist is to confuse a cashier by requesting several types of transactions at the same time.

10. In the event of an error or misring on the register, the total amount of the ring should be recorded on a cashier's correction sheet. The entire transaction is then rung again—this time, correctly. Cashiers should not try to deduct or adjust on a subsequent transaction. Splitting rings or bunching should also be discouraged. Each transaction should be rung separately and correctly, just as it appears on the guest check. Completed checks should then be register validated.

11. Making payments out of the cash drawer is a practice auditors and tax agents frown upon. The only paid-outs that are considered legitimate are payments to service staff for tips charged on credit cards or house accounts. These payments should be itemized on a waiter's tip sheet and signed for by each waiter when he receives his tips at the end of each serving period. This signed form then becomes part of the cashier's closing documentation.

12. Closing procedures should include the following:

   a. The cashier should count the total receipts and prepare his bank for the following day. The remaining cash constitutes his deposit for the shift. This should be counted by denomination (quarters, nickels, single dollars, fives, and so forth) and the amounts entered on a cashier's deposit slip or envelope (see fig. 17-1).

   b. The cashier also prepares a daily report showing the amount of cash and charge sales, tips paid out, and other pertinent data (see fig. 17-2).

   c. The cashier's deposit and report are then turned over to the manager or (in a large operation) to a head cashier or member of the accounting staff. For his own protection, the cashier should have a record book or receive a receipt containing the amount of the deposit, the date, and the signature of the person who received the deposit. If the operation has a safe with a drop slot, the cashier should have a witness when making the drop. This witness and the cashier should then sign the record book.

17-1. Cashier's deposit envelope.

    d. In some operations, the cashier's deposit becomes the bank deposit. In this case, the cashier would also prepare the bank deposit slips. Even if the manager does not choose to go to the bank every day, each day's deposit should be kept separate and intact, amounting to the total day's cash sales (minus any tips paid out). This provides an audit trail for future reference.

13. Register readings should be taken by someone other than the cashier. Registers should not be reset; the readings should continue from one day to the next. The difference

DAILY SALES REPORT			DATE:						SALES TX.	PREPARED BY:			TOTAL
			REGISTER #1		REGISTER #2		REGISTER #3						TOTAL
			READINGS	TOTAL	READINGS	TOTAL	READINGS	TOTAL	ADJ.				SALES
1	FOOD	END									FOOD		
2		BEG											
3	BEER	END									BEER		
4	WINE	BEG									WINE		
5	LIQUOR	END									LIQUOR		
6		BEG											
7	TAX	END									TAX		
8		BEG											
9	TIP	END									TIP		
10		BEG											
11													
12													
13	TOTAL SALES										TOTAL SALES		

			CASH A	CASH B	CASH A	CASH B	CASH A	CASH B				
14	CASH	END										
15		BEG										
16	SUB-TOTAL											
17	ADJUSTMENTS											
18	TOTAL											
19	CHARGE	END										
20		BEG										
21	SUB-TOTAL											
22	ADJUSTMENTS											
23	TOTAL										*CHARGE	
24	TIPS PAID										TIPS PAID	
25												
26												
27	ACCT'D FOR										ACCT'D FOR	
28	DEPOSIT										DEPOSIT	
29	(OVER) SHORT										(OV) SHORT	

SUMMARY RESTAURANT	LUNCH	DINNER	TOTAL	COMMENTS:	* CHARGES SUMMARY	
FOOD					HOUSE CHARGE	$
BEER/WINE					AMERICAN EXPRESS	
LIQUOR					DINERS CLUB	
TOTAL					CARTE BLANCHE	
					MASTER CHARGE	
					BANKAMERICARD	
COVERS						
AVG. FOOD						
AVG. BEV.						
COMBINED					TOTAL	

17-2. Cashier's report form.

between the opening and closing readings should agree with the amount shown on the cashier's daily report. It should be adjusted for any amounts on the cashier's error sheet. If not, the cashier is either "over" or "short."

ELECTRONIC POINT-OF-SALE REGISTERS

Electronic point-of-sale equipment can provide much of the information on the daily report automatically. In addition, it can

```
----------------------------------------------
              GUEST CHECK
  SERVER   120 TABLE    25/ 1   TIME  16:24

    1 GIBSON/STOLY            3.00
    1 MANHATTAN-RYE           3.00
    1 BUCKET/MUSSL            3.95
    1 SOUP DJ/BOWL            1.75
    1 LOBSTER SALAD           5.50
    1 BR SCALLOPS             6.95
    1 BLACK REDFISH          10.95
    1 APPLE PIE ALA           2.75
    1 CHEESECAKE              2.25
    2 COFFEE                  1.00
                          --------

              TOTAL          41.10
                TAX           2.11
      PAID BY AMEX          -43.21 TIP   9.00
                          --------
          GRAND TOTAL         NIL

      AMEX NUMBER 1234567890


      THANK YOU FOR DINING WITH US!
  HAVING A PARTY - PERHAPS WE CAN HELP
             297 - 3803


    86-12-09     2 GUESTS   NUMBER      2
----------------------------------------------
```

17-3. A guest check produced by a Remanco point-of-sale system. (Courtesy of Remanco Systems, Inc. and Mega Computer Systems.)

produce reports showing information by server, by time period, by menu item, and by sales outlet. It can also function as a time clock, and it can produce payroll and labor cost reports. Figures 17-3 through 17-7 show sample reports from a point-of-sale system.

```
                    ***************
                   *  CASH  REPORT  *
                    ***************


                PRINTED ON: 86-12-09    AT: 14:46

                            CURRENT      PERIOD TO DATE
          NUMBER OF CHECKS:    128          128
          NUMBER OF GUESTS:    328          328

        CONFIGURATION FILE: HH1   .CON   MENU FILE: SMEN24.MEN
        TRAIL FILE: 61123 .TRL          CHECK FILE: 61123 .CHK

        NUMBER OF ACCUMULATED FILES THIS REPORT:    1

   FILE NAME    START TIME   FINISH TIME   FIRST CHECK  LAST CHECK   DATE OF FILE
    61123         22:02        7:36             1          123        86-11-23

                    ********************
```

SUMMARY BY SALES CATEGORY:	SALES CATEGORY IDENTIFICATION	CURRENT AMOUNT	PERIOD TO DATE
	BEVERAGES	130.00	130.00
	SANDWICHES	515.70	515.70
	SALADS	77.00	77.00
	BURGERS	167.45	167.45
	LUNCHEONS	29.70	29.70
	APPETIZERS	206.40	206.40
	SOUPS	64.75	64.75
	SIDE ORDERS	54.00	54.00
	ENTREES	1944.75	1944.75
	DESSERTS	116.50	116.50
	BEER	198.00	198.00
	LIQUOR	167.75	167.75
	WINE	56.25	56.25
	BOTTLED WINE	23.70	23.70
	SPECIALITY DRINKS	42.00	42.00
	INTL COFFEES	6.00	6.00
	COFFEES	72.00	72.00
	MISC	35.40	35.40
	TOTAL:	3907.35	3907.35
	TOTAL TAX:	204.92	204.92
	TOTAL SALES:	4112.27	4112.27

TAX CATEGORY ANALYSIS:	TOTAL-	CURRENT	PERIOD TO DATE
	FOOD:	204.92	204.92
	BEER:	0.00	0.00
	LIQUOR:	0.00	0.00
	WINE:	0.00	0.00
	SERVICE CHARGE:	0.00	0.00
	ENTERTAINMENT:	0.00	0.00
	TOTAL TAX:	204.92	204.92

```
VOIDS AFFECTING INVENTORY: LIQUOR                 3.50         3.50


TOTAL VOIDS (NO OPTIONS)
  NOT AFFECTING INVENTORY:        NUMBER OF VOIDS:   30           30
                                          VALUE:  105.75       105.75


TIP ANALYSIS:    DECLARED CASH TIPS (NO OPTIONS):  268.00       268.00
                                    CHARGE TIPS:  140.14       140.14

                                         TOTAL:  408.14       408.14

              PERCENTAGE TIPS OF TOTAL SALES:       9.92         9.92


                    ********************
```

17-4. A daily cash report produced by a Remanco point-of-sale system. (Courtesy of Remanco Systems, Inc. and Mega Computer Systems.)

```
SUMMARY BY PAYMENT METHOD:           PAYMENT        CURRENT      PERIOD
                                  IDENTIFICATION     AMOUNT      TO DATE
                                  --------------    --------    --------
         UNREVISED:     83 CASH                     2769.11     2769.11
                         9 VISA/MASTERCARD           385.19      385.19
                        16 AMERICAN EXPRESS          633.66      633.66
                         1 HOUSE ACCOUNTS              5.50        5.50
                        20 COUPONS                   232.25      232.25
                        19 EMPLOYEE MEALS             86.56       86.56
                                                   --------    --------
                        TOTAL:                      4112.27     4112.27
                                                   ========    ========

                        NOTE:           CASH:       2909.25     2909.25
                               LESS CHARGE TIPS:      140.14      140.14
                                                   --------    --------
                                    NET CASH:        2769.11     2769.11
                                                   ========    ========


                        ********************
```

17-4. *(Continued)*


```
                                                           PAGE   1
                       ****************
                     *  TIP  REPORT  *
                       ****************

                   PRINTED ON:86-12-09    AT:16:00

                   REPORT BY CHECK CREATION SERVER

                   CHECK FILENAME   TABLE NUMBER(S)
                       61123
```

ID#	TOTAL RECEIPTS	SRV.INC. TOTAL RECEIPTS	%SRV. CHRG.	CHARGE RECEIPTS WITH TIP	CHARGE TIPS	CASH RECEIPTS	REPORTED CASH TIPS	TOTAL TIPS	%TIP/ TOTAL RECEIPTS
135	123.60	0.00	0.00	44.00	7.00	79.60	4.00	11.00	8.90
112	1001.07	0.00	0.00	633.70	86.07	367.37	10.00	96.07	9.60
150	319.55	0.00	0.00	9.30	0.00	310.25	33.00	33.00	10.33
123	661.35	0.00	0.00	100.30	8.00	561.05	61.00	69.00	10.43
118	824.60	0.00	0.00	136.13	13.00	688.47	72.00	85.00	10.31
130	123.10	0.00	0.00	11.00	0.00	112.10	12.00	12.00	9.75
117	331.80	0.00	0.00	78.85	0.00	252.95	34.00	34.00	10.25
133	372.97	0.00	0.00	179.77	21.52	193.20	16.00	37.52	10.06
111	289.45	0.00	0.00	71.03	4.55	218.42	26.00	30.55	10.55

```
            ********************** TOTALS **********************
            TOTAL RECEIPTS                                4047.49
            SERVICE CHARGE INCLUDED IN TOTAL RECEIPTS        0.00
            CHARGE RECEIPTS WITH TIPS                     1264.08
            CHARGE TIPS                                    140.14
            CASH RECEIPTS                                 2783.41
            REPORTED CASH TIPS                             268.00
            TOTAL TIPS                                     408.14
            % TIPS/TOTAL RECEIPTS                           10.08
```

17-5. A tip report produced by a Remanco point-of-sale system. (Courtesy of Remanco Systems, Inc. and Mega Computer Systems.)

```
DATE:86-12-09                          PAGE:   1

      ****************************************
      *DAILY  CASH  RECONCILIATION  REPORT*
      ****************************************


                 NUMBER OF CHECKS:   256
                 NUMBER OF GUESTS:   330

                 MENU FILE: SMEN24.MEN
       CHECK FILE: 61123 .CHK      TRAIL FILE: 61123 .TRL
            PERSONNEL FILE: SPER4 .PER

            AVERAGE CHECK BY GUEST VERSION

OPTION  INFORMATION:
#########################

OPTION NUMBER:  0  IDENTIFIER: DAILY SALES

SERVER  SALES:
###################
```

SERVER NAME	ID# ---	INCOME $	OVER/ SHORT	ENTREES Q/D	APPETIZERS Q/D	PREM GL/WI Q/D	SIDE ORDER Q/D	DESSERTS Q/D	OTHER ITEMS	GUESTS $S/AVER
STEVE ; FALLON	111	300.79	( )	29	7	0	5	4	44	28
			--------	228.45	22.35	0.00	7.00	5.50	42.50	305.80
			$/GUEST	8.16	0.80	0.00	0.25	0.20	1.52	10.93
			%MIX	104.00	25.00	0.00	18.00	14.00	157.00	########
KEVIN ; MCDONALD	112	963.76	( )	92	25	2	9	19	128	81
			--------	626.65	76.85	5.50	12.75	39.50	145.75	907.00
- H I G H S A L E S *-*			$/GUEST	7.74	0.95	0.07	0.16	0.49	1.80	11.21
			%MIX	114.00	31.00	2.00	11.00	23.00	158.00	########
DEBRA ; GROSSMAN	150	333.85	( )	26	0	0	0	0	41	25
			--------	221.00	0.00	0.00	0.00	0.00	89.25	310.25
			$/GUEST	8.84	0.00	0.00	0.00	0.00	3.57	12.41
			%MIX	104.00	0.00	0.00	0.00	0.00	164.00	########

```
TOTAL SERVER INCOME DOLLARS----> 4112.27
```

17-6. A server productivity report produced by a Remanco point-of-sale system. (Courtesy of Remanco Systems, Inc. and Mega Computer Systems.)

```
                                                         PAGE:    1
                        TCARD  REPORT
                        ***********

                PRINTED ON: 86-12-09  AT: 16:07:50
                AUDIT TRAIL FILENAME: 61123.TRL
                AUDIT TRAIL CREATION: 86-11-23
--------------------------------------------------------------------
 NAME:  STEVE      FALLON           PERSONNEL #: 122
--------------------------------------------------------------------
  DATE    CLOCK   DATE    CLOCK ID#  JOB   PAY   HOURS  TOTAL   TIPS      PAY
  IN      IN      OUT     OUT        CLASS RATE         HOURS
--------------------------------------------------------------------
 86-11-24 00:46 86-11-24 06:54 111    3  2.010  6.13                30.55    12.33
                                                     6.13
                                                     ------           ---------
                                                     6.13                     12.33
--------------------------------------------------------------------



 NAME:  KEVIN     MCDONALD         PERSONNEL #: 143
--------------------------------------------------------------------
  DATE    CLOCK   DATE    CLOCK ID#  JOB   PAY   HOURS  TOTAL   TIPS      PAY
  IN      IN      OUT     OUT        CLASS RATE         HOURS
--------------------------------------------------------------------
 86-11-23 20:30 86-11-24 07:35 112    3  2.010  11.08               96.07    22.28
                                                     11.08
                                                     ------           ---------
                                                     11.08                    22.28
--------------------------------------------------------------------
```

17-7. Time cards produced by a Remanco point-of-sale system. (Courtesy of Remanco Systems, Inc. and Mega Computer Systems.)

SECURITY OF CASH AND MERCHANDISE

There are four classes of thefts—thefts by others (robberies), thefts by customers, thefts by cashiers, and thefts by waiters.

Customer stealing can be accomplished through:

- Short-change artists
- Walkouts
- Counterfeit or altered money
- Credit card fraud
- Bad checks

Dishonest cashiers have developed various techniques, including:

- Shortchanging customers

- Not ringing up exact change sales
- Ringing up sales at less than the full amount, permitting an overage that is subsequently removed from the drawer

Waiters, too, have specific tricks for stealing:

- Not charging for food or drinks served
- Not turning in all funds collected to the cashier
- Overcharging guests and turning in the correct amount
- Pricing checks incorrectly
- Misusing checks or dupes to obtain extra food from the kitchen for themselves or their friends

Robberies

The experts are unanimous in their advice in handling robberies. Do not try to be a hero; you may be a dead hero. The Continental Illinois National Bank advises that you follow the procedures below.[1]

If you are robbed, do not resist! Money is replaceable; human life is not. Since many robbers are nervous amateurs or desperate drug addicts in need of quick money to support their habit, resistance may lead to injury or death.

To help apprehend and successfully prosecute a robber, victims and other witnesses to the robbery must be able to identify an offender and link him to a criminal act. Remembering the personal characteristics of the robber (fig. 17-8) as well as the other items listed below will aid in later apprehension, identification, and conviction:

1. Body build (thin, medium, or stocky); height and weight.
2. Any readily distinguishable marks, scars, tattoos, or deformities.
3. The color and style of the robber's hair, his facial characteristics and complexion, whether he has a beard or mustache, and the color of his eyes.
4. Type of clothes the robber was wearing.

[1]*Businessman's Guide to Protection Against Crime,* Continental Illinois Bank and Trust Company of Chicago, 1974.

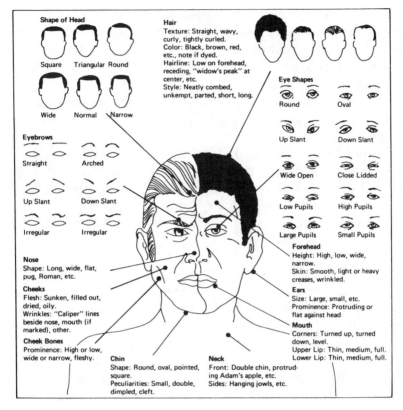

17-8. Personal characteristics of a robber. (Courtesy of Continental Illinois Bank.)

5. Peculiarities—distinguishable mannerisms, accent, limp, or other distinguishing physical characteristics.
6. Type, color, size, and shape of weapon.
7. Mode and direction of escape—if by car, get a description of the car, its license number, and, when possible, a description of the driver if the robbery was a two-person job.
8. Type of receptacle the money or goods were placed in, i.e., paper bag, cloth bag.

Call the police as soon as it is safe. Tell them where the robbery occurred, when it occurred, and the mode and direction of flight. Encourage witnesses to remain and refrain from talking with one another about the crime until the police have arrived. Do not move or even handle any items that the robbers may have touched or disturb any evidence.

You can reduce your chances of being robbed. Question suspicious persons loitering about the premises. Have training sessions with the staff to make them security conscious too. If enough people ask questions, a potential robber may go elsewhere.

Do not keep large amounts of cash on the premises, and do not count money in a public area. Take it to a secure office, away from view. If you have a robbery, do not immediately report the amount taken. A large amount reported in the press may attract more robbers in the future.

Short-Change Artists

The short-change artist is a professional. He counts on carelessness and inattentiveness by the cashier to pull off his act. When the customer pays the waiter, this thief has much less opportunity to rob. However, he may claim to have given the waiter a larger denomination bill than was actually rendered. Waiters should be trained to enter on the check the amount of money received and to verbally acknowledge the amount to the guest.

When customers pay cashiers, it is a different story. Cashiers should be trained to be alert to the short-change artist. Concentration and careful adherence to the correct cashiering procedures are the only way to thwart this individual.

Walkouts

A walkout is a customer who leaves without paying his check. This type of loss can be reduced by an alert staff. Where customers pay the waiter, it is definitely the responsibility of the service staff to see that all checks are settled. When waiters work in teams, one member should always be on the station, alert to any guests who look like they are going to take a walk. When waiters work singly, it is more difficult to prevent a walkout, but captains and supervisors should always be on the lookout.

Walkouts are more prevalent when customers pay the cashier directly. It becomes quite easy to mingle with a group of people paying at the door and slip out undetected. Under no circumstances should a cashier leave the cash station to chase a walkout. He should call the manager. If the losses from walkouts become significant, it may be a good idea to have a manager stationed near the door during busy periods.

The physical layout of the restaurant may also contribute to walkouts. If there is a secondary exit from the dining room, some means of securing it may be necessary. Also, a second cashier stand may be required during busy periods.

Handling a walkout is touchy. Some walkouts are unintentional; the customer may be absentminded or engaged in conversation. A tactful reminder to the departing guest should be the first step. Usually, this is sufficient. If the customer is out the door, it is not advisable to try to chase him. You are outside of your own premises, and the individual could turn and harm you. The customers still in the dining room are your primary responsibility.

Counterfeit or Altered Money

Anyone who handles cash should be trained to detect counterfeit or altered money. If any of these bills are accepted, the restaurant is stuck. Bad bills are usually of a large denomination, such as twenties and fifties. They often run in spurts, and the local police may put out an alert that bad bills are being passed in the community.

Counterfeit money has a different feel to it. A bill that does not seem quite right, especially a large denomination, should be examined carefully. Tiny blue and red hairs should be embedded in the paper; counterfeit bills will not have these lines. (A good strong light is needed on the cashier's station for such an examination.) Also, the points on the seal should be distinct and clear with no broken or missing points. Smudged background on the portrait and blurred details or broken lines on the border design are also indications of "funny" money.

A genuine bill may also be altered to raise the denomination. Take a careful look at all large bills, front and back, to be sure that they have not been altered.

Credit Card Fraud

Credit cards are a fact of life these days, and most table service restaurants honor them. You should instruct cashiers and waiters to proceed as follows when handling a credit card transaction:

1. Check the expiration date to see if the card is still valid.
2. Compare the signature on the charge ticket with that on the card to see if they are the same.
3. Card companies publish lists of stolen, lost, or canceled cards. Check to see if the card is on the current list. If it is and you accept the charge, you can be stuck for the total amount of the bill.
4. Card companies also have a floor limit. All transactions above this amount must be cleared by telephone call with the credit card company, even if the card number is not on the blacklist. The amount of the floor limit varies according to the company and the type of restaurant.
5. If there is any doubt about the validity of the credit card or if it appears to have been altered or defaced, ask for additional identification. Get the customer to sign the guest check and compare signatures.
6. If there is any indication of foul play, detain the customer and call the manager.

Checking lists for a large number of transactions can slow down the cashier considerably. Credit card companies have available small computer terminals that will automatically check the validity of the card while imprinting the card voucher.

Bad Checks

Payment by check is not as common in restaurants as payment by credit card. However, many restaurants will accept a check as a last resort to collect from a customer. To reduce the exposure to risk, the Continental Bank advises the following steps in handling a check transaction:[2]

[2] *Businessman's Guide to Protection Against Crime,* Continental Illinois Bank and Trust Company of Chicago, 1974.

1. Read the check face and back. It should look like a check. Some stores have cashed telephone bills paying the amount due on the bill. Record vouchers or advertising devices also have been presented as bona fide checks and cashed.
2. A check must be properly made out:
   - If it is a personal check payable to the store or establishment, it should bear the date it is cashed (within two or three days of cashing).
   - The writer's name and address should be imprinted on the face of the check.
   - It should be made out to the store or establishment cashing it.
   - The amount in numbers should be identical to the spelled-out amount.
   - The bank's name and address should be imprinted on the check.
   - The signature of the maker should be legible, as should all writing on the check.
3. The check should not show signs of erasures or alterations; if either is present, the check should not be cashed.
4. Identification should be required. Certain types of identification that are hard to steal or duplicate bear the name and description of the person to whom they are issued, or demonstrate that the individual's credit-worthiness has been previously determined. Only these forms of identification should be used to determine whether to cash a check, but even then it is best to ask for two or three. Examples include a valid driver's license, an employee I.D. card bearing a picture, or a store's own credit card if it has a signature.
   - The description on the identification card ("I.D.") should be carefully checked to make sure that it matches the appearance of the person cashing the check.
   - The signature on the I.D. should be compared with that of the person cashing the check.
   - The name, address, and phone number on the check should match that on the I.D.
   - The type of I.D. presented and the physical description of the person cashing the check should be noted on the back of the check.

- The check should be reendorsed in the cashier's presence if there is doubt that the check passer signed the check originally. Often a forger will not be able to spell even the name of the payee or to duplicate the previous endorsement.
- Remember, check cashing is a courtesy; there is no obligation to cash any check. But keep in mind too that it is an integral and necessary part of the transfer of funds process.

Thefts by Cashiers and Waiters

These types of thefts may victimize the customer as well as the restaurant. Cashier thefts include pocketing the amount of an exact change transaction and destroying the check or ringing up less than the amount of the check and taking the difference. Another type of cashier theft is short-changing the guest. With waiters, theft techniques include swinging checks; that is, using the same check to collect from several customers and only turning in the last collection, or using another customer's check to overcharge a guest and turning in the correct check and amount; altering checks to overcharge the guest and then turning in the correct amount; not charging for certain items in hopes of getting a bigger tip; and (intentionally or unintentionally) pricing or adding incorrectly.

These types of theft can be minimized by the following techniques:

1. The first defense is a good offense. Check carefully the people hired. Have all cashiers and people handling money bonded. The bonding company's security check is very helpful.
2. Investigate any cashier who works with the drawer open; who works with a note pad with scribbled numbers; or who frequently rings up no sales, voids checks, or splits amounts.
3. Make a policy that no erasures are permitted on checks and that any check on which the amount is changed must be approved by a supervisor.
4. Review the guest checks periodically for indications of era-

sures, misrings, improper pricing and totaling, or improper or missing validation marks from the cash settlement register.

5. Where counter attendants and bartenders collect their own checks and ring them up, provide a locked drop box with a slot for closed checks and require the server to deposit each check in the box as soon as the transaction is completed.

6. Use spotters from an outside shopper service to check on the waiter and cashier procedures being used.

7. From time to time, pull the cashier's drawer in the middle of service. Have a supervisor step in and cover the station while you and the cashier count the amount collected in the till. Investigate any large overages or shortages in the cash count at that time. Let your cashiers know that you will be doing this as a matter of routine. An honest cashier will not mind.

8. Require that all prices be imprinted on the checks by machine. Do not permit prices to be penciled in on the checks.

9. Account for all missing checks on a daily basis and keep all reserve checks locked up.

10. Provide adding machines and insist that waiters use them to total checks if they are not machine totaled.

11. Consider the use of electronic point-of-sale register equipment.

12. Match up guest checks with the dupes from the kitchen (if they are used) on a test basis.

13. Time stamp checks at the range in the kitchen and at the time of settlement. Spot check how long the check was open. An unreasonable span of time may mean it was used for more than one transaction.

14. Employees with positive attitudes and close identification with their employer seldom steal. Work toward establishing a good morale by paying fair rates and treating the employees as an important part of the team (which, of course, they are).

15. Fire anyone caught stealing, regardless of the amount. One bad apple can spoil the bunch. It is not a matter of how

much was stolen but the fact that it was stolen. Establish this policy quickly and follow through.

16. Law enforcement agencies encourage managers to prosecute all persons caught stealing (regardless of the amount) as a deterrent to others. If the offender is a young person in his first job, you must follow your own conscience as to whether pressing charges is warranted.

THE CASHIER AND THE PUBLIC

The cashier who deals directly with the customer is the last person to see the guest before he leaves the restaurant. A guest who has a complaint often will not register it until he has to part with his cash. For this reason, cashiers often hear complaints and should not pass them over lightly. *The cashier should never let a dissatisfied guest leave the restaurant.*

At the point of payment, it is too late to correct a problem with the meal or service, but the situation may be saved by offering a future meal, a drink, or bottle of wine, or by deducting something from the check. These gestures must be made by a supervisor or manager, however, and not by a cashier. If a supervisor is not available, or if the guest does not want to wait, the cashier should get his name and telephone number or address so that a call or letter can subsequently be sent. Failing all else, the cashier should note the complaint, apologize graciously, and report it to the supervisor or manager as soon as possible. A delay in correcting a problem could mean that other guests may be dissatisfied.

As with all other front of the house personnel, cashiers need to be well groomed and pleasant mannered. Having a good telephone voice is important since answering the phone is usually part of their duties. Cashiers should also have a good knowledge of the neighborhood and happenings around town since they are apt to be asked questions and directions by departing guests.

Bibliography and Training Materials

BOOKS

Service

Cornell University, School of Hotel Administration. "The Essentials of Good Table Service." *The Cornell Hotel and Restaurant Administration Quarterly,* Ithaca, NY: 1971.

Dahmer, Sondra J., and Kahl, Kurt W. *The Waiter and Waitress Training Manual.* 2d. ed. New York: Van Nostrand Reinhold Company, 1982.

Durocher, Joseph F., and Goodman, Raymond J., Jr. *The Essentials of Tableside Cookery.* Cornell University, School of Hotel Administration. No date.

The Foodservice Editors of CBI. *The Professional Host.* New York: Van Nostrand Reinhold Company, 1980.

Ginders, James. *A Guide to Napkin Folding.* New York: Van Nostrand Reinhold Company, 1980.

Lillicrap, D. R. *Food and Beverage Service.* London: Edward Arnold Publishers, 1983.

Mulcahy, Cherie, and Corbin, Robert. *Today's Busperson.* New York: Lebhar-Friedman Books, 1979.

———. *Today's Cocktail Waitress.* New York: Lebhar-Friedman Books, 1979.

———. *Today's Waiter and Waitress.* New York: Lebhar-Friedman Books, 1979.

Food References

Bickel, Walter. *Hering's Dictionary of Classical and Modern Cookery.* 5th rev. English ed. New York: Van Nostrand Reinhold Company, 1974.

Wasserman, Pauline, with Wasserman, Sheldon. *Don't Ask Your Waiter.* Briarcliffe Manor, NY: Stein & Day, 1980.

Restaurant Management and Supervision

Birchfield, John C. *Foodservice Operations Manual.* New York: Van Nostrand Reinhold Company, 1979.

Green, Eric; Drake, Galen; and Sweeney, Jerome. *Profitable Food and Beverage Management: Operations.* Rochelle Park, NJ: Hayden Book Company, 1978.

————. *Profitable Food and Beverage Management: Planning.* Rochelle Park, NJ: Hayden Book Company, 1978.

Kasavana, Michael L. *Computer Systems for Foodservice Operations.* New York: Van Nostrand Reinhold Company, 1984.

McIntosh, Robert W. *Employee Management Standards.* New York: Van Nostrand Reinhold Company, 1984.

Miller, Jack. *Supervision in the Hospitality Industry.* New York: John Wiley & Sons, 1985.

Ninemeier, Jack D. *Food and Beverage Security.* New York: Van Nostrand Reinhold Company, 1982.

Schmidt, Arno B. *The Banquet Business.* New York: Van Nostrand Reinhold Company, 1980.

Stokes, Arch. *The Equal Opportunity Handbook for Hotels, Restaurants, and Institutions.* New York: Van Nostrand Reinhold Company, 1979.

Wines and Beverages

Grossman, Harold J. *Grossman's Guide to Wines, Spirits, and Beers.* New York: Charles Scribner's Sons, 1974.

Katsigris, Costas, and Porter, Mary. *The Bar and Beverage Book: Basics of Profitable Management.* New York: John Wiley & Sons, 1983.

Lichine, Alexis. *New Encyclopedia of Wines and Spirits*. New York: Alfred A. Knopf, 1974.

Moore, Philip. *Total Bar and Beverage Management*. New York: Lebhar-Friedman Books, 1981.

HOME STUDY COURSES

American Hotel & Motel Association
888 Seventh Avenue
New York, NY 10106

National Institute for the Food Service Industry
20 North Wacker Drive
Suite 2620
Chicago, IL 60606

Purdue University
Continuing Education Program
Room 110, Stewart Center
West Lafayette, IN 47907

TRAINING MATERIALS AND PROGRAMS

American Hotel & Motel Association
888 Seventh Avenue
New York, NY 10106
(Educational Institute; *Lodging* magazine)

Brymer Video Penthouse
533 Yates Street
Victoria, British Columbia,
Canada V8W 1K7
(Video)

Continental Film Products Corporation
Box 5126
Chattanooga, TN 37406
(Video)

The Culinary Institute of America
Hyde Park, NY 12538
(Video)

National Educational Media, Inc. (NEM)
21601 Devonshire Street
Chatsworth, CA 91311
(Video)

National Restaurant Association
311 First Street N.W.
Washington, DC 20001
(Catalog of publications)

Prentice-Hall Media
Box 1050
Mount Kisco, NY 10549-9989
(Video)

The Qualityservice Group
Box 2068
Princeton, NJ 08540
(Professional Hospitality Skills training program)

Responsible Hospitality Institute
11 Pearl Street, Suite 226
Springfield, MA 01105
(Responsible beverage service materials)

Textile Rental Services Association of America
Box 1283
1250 East Hallandale Beach Boulevard
Hallandale, FL 33009
(Video)

Index

Page numbers in *italic* indicate illustrations.

Abboyeur, 27
Abdicative leader, 116
Accidents, 45
Advertising materials, 92–93
Age Discrimination in Employment Act, 82, 148
Aggression response, 126
Alcohol lamp, 6
Altered money, 199
Alternative behavior, 126
American formal setting, 35
American service, 7–8, *9*
Arbitration, 158–59
Arm service, 13
Attitudes, 128–29
Authoritarian leader, 117, 124
Authority, 115

Bad checks, 200–201
Banquet service standards, 41–42
Bar service, 50–56, *52, 54*
Beer, pouring technique, 53–54
Behavioral skills training, 137
Beverage service standards, 49–50
   bar service, 50–56, *52, 54*
   responsible service, 60–64
   wine service, 56–59, *58*

Blind guests, 103–4
Blood alcohol concentration (BAC), 61
Body language, 99–100, *99*
Bona fide occupational qualification, 147–48
Breakage, 72, *73*
Breakdowns (service), 43–45
Buddy system, 132–33
Buffet service, 8, *9,* 10
   standards of, 42–43
Busboys, 16
Butler service, 10, *11*

Call brand, 50
Captains, 16
Cart, 6
Cart service, 12
Cashiering and revenue control, 183
   cashier and the public, 204
   cashiering procedures, 186–89, *189, 190*
   common control systems, 184–86
   point-of-sale registers, 190, *191–95*
   security measures, 194–203, *197*
Checker system, 184
Checklists, 22, *23–24*